Editor, Tom Finley
Consulting Editors,
    Marian Wiggins
    Annette Parrish
Contributing Writers
    Rick Bundschuh
    Carol Bostrom
    Sandy and Dale Larsen
Designed and Illustrated by Tom Finley

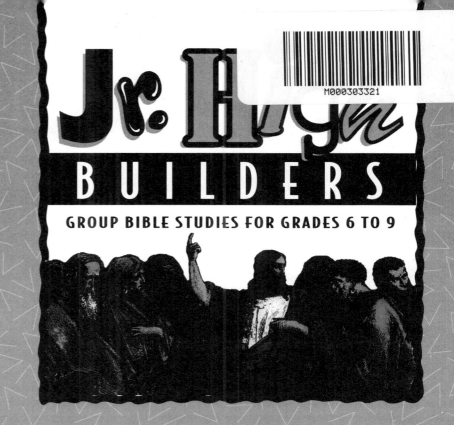

Jr. High BUILDERS

GROUP BIBLE STUDIES FOR GRADES 6 TO 9

CHRISTIAN RELATIONSHIPS

MY RELATIONSHIP WITH GOD, MYSELF AND WITH OTHERS

NUMBER 5 IN A SERIES OF 12

Gospel Light

INTRODUCTION

This book contains everything you need to teach any size group of junior high students about three important areas of Christian relationships: with God, with ourselves and with others. Thirteen sessions, with complete session plans for the leader, reproducible classroom worksheets and reproducible take-home papers. Also, thirteen lecture-oriented Bible study outlines based on the same themes, to provide your students with needed reinforcement from a fresh perspective. And—dozens of action games and ideas to round out your youth program, plus a special section of clip art featuring illustrations to promote your Bible studies and dress up your announcement handbills.

Contents

Bible Studies:

OVERVIEW
OF THE PARTS AND PIECES

There is a ton of great teaching tools in this book, including object lessons, Bible games, memory verses, discussion questions, stories, worksheets, comic cartoons and more! Here's an overview of it all:

The **SESSION PLAN** contains two essential ingredients for a meaningful Bible study all students will enjoy: a commentary section to provide the leader with important biblical information and to set the stage for the lesson; and a lesson plan filled with Bible Learning Activities to help students retain spiritual truths. **FOR A DETAILED DESCRIPTION, TURN TO PAGE 6.**

The **STUDENT WORKSHEET,** called the **Gateway,** allows the student to learn by doing rather than just sitting and listening. Photocopy as many sheets as you need. **SEE PAGE 8 FOR COMPLETE DETAILS.**

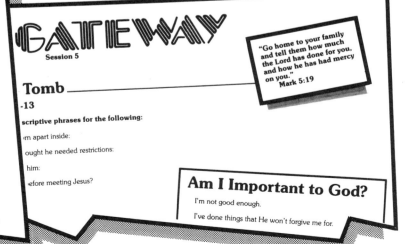

Wise Living
SESSION 6

INSIGHTS FOR THE LEADER

WHAT THE SESSION IS ABOUT

We need God's wisdom in order to make the right decisions in life.

SCRIPTURE STUDIED

Psalm 14:1; Proverbs 1:7; 2:6,7; 3:5,6; 14:9; 16:7; 19:8; 29:9,11; Matthew 7:24-29; Romans 1:21,22; 1 Corinthians 10:12; Galatians 6:3; Titus 3:3; James 1:5; 3:13-18.

KEY PASSAGE

"If any of you lacks wisdom, he should ask God, who gives ... without finding ... given to him."

If confusion about who they are, what values they should hold, and what feelings they should experience is the ailment of typical junior highers, then the wisdom to do the right thing is the needed cure. Unfortunately, it is noticeably lacking in the lives of most people.

Wisdom is not a very popular commodity in the youth world. It is confused with visions of craggy, white-haired old men sitting in brooding silence and occasionally proclaiming a great insight (for those who have the patience to sit around long enough to hear it). Wisdom is equated with age and experience, and does not appear to kids to be attainable or particularly desirable.

The truth of the matter is that wisdom is what all people need, no matter what their age. It is the focal point of maturity, the catalyst for good thinking, the anchor in the swirling ... of modern thought. ... struggle of choosing ...

and everyday, involving the ability to understand God's truth and apply it to daily life. It is often vividly contrasted in Scripture with its opposite—foolishness.

The biblical picture indicates that everyone is moving toward becoming wise or becoming foolish. There does not appear to be much middle ground. Scripture tells us that true wisdom comes only from God (see Prov. 1:7; 2:6,7) and that it is directly related to how we obey His Word. Proverbs 3:5,6 says, "Lean not on your own understanding; in all your ways acknowledge him, and he will make your paths straight."

In stark contrast, the Bible states, "The fool says in his heart, 'There is no God'" (Ps. 14:1).

The Builders

Our need for God's wisdom is most keenly felt during times of confusion ... problems. ... described ...

GATEWAY
Session 5

"Go home to your family and tell them how much the Lord has done for you, and how he has had mercy on you."
Mark 5:19

____ Tomb ____
-13

... scriptive phrases for the following:

... rn apart inside:

... ought he needed restrictions:

... him:

... efore meeting Jesus?

Am I Important to God?

I'm not good enough.

I've done things that He won't forgive me for.

4

The **TEACHING RESOURCE PAGE** provides special items such as short stories or case studies when required by the **Session Plan.** Most **Session Plans** have no **Teaching Resource Page.** FOR DETAILS, SEE PAGE 9.

The **TAKE-HOME PAPER,** called the **Fun Page,** features a Bible game (such as a maze or crossword), comic strip or short story, daily devotional questions and a memory verse for motivated students. **FOR MORE ABOUT THE FUN PAGE, TURN TO PAGE 10.**

The Matching Maze

The qualities listed on the left side of this page are things that make a person happy, content, joyous and successful on the inside (where it really counts). Match the qualities that result from seeking God first with the Scripture (on the right side of the page) that deals with the listed qualities. Then use a pencil to draw lines through the maze to connect the passages with their matching qualities. But you can't cross your own line (except on paths that obviously pass over or under each other) and you can't use the same section of path twice. Use a pencil (with a big eraser).

Qualities:

Good name (or reputation)

Humility

Pure

Steadfast (reliable, steady) or strong

Bible Passages:

James 1:5

Proverbs 22:1

Proverbs 21:21

1 John 3:3

Proverbs 22:4

Ephesians 6:10

"VEIG, AND IT LIWL BE EIGNV TO YOU. A DOGO SEREMAU, DSSEERP WOND, AENKHS RHETTEOG AND GNUNINR EVRO, ILWL BE DPOEUR TOIN OUYR ALP. RFO TWHI THE UAMEERS UYO EUS, IT WILL BE AUMESEDR OT UYO."

DAILY NUGGETS

Day 1 Read Acts 20:35. What could you give to another this week?

Day 2 Ephesians 5:2. What does this verse say that Christ has given for us?

Day 3 Luke 16:19-31. What could the rich man have done for Lazarus? What did the rich man want Lazarus to do for him?

Day 4 John 13:14,15. What is the meaning of the example Christ provided?

Day 5 1 John 2:10. How could a Christian cause another person to stumble or trip up in his or her spiritual life?

Day 6 1 Corinthians 10:24. Whose good should we seek?

"One man gives freely, yet gains even more; another withholds unduly, but comes to poverty. A generous man will prosper; he who refreshes others will himself be refreshed." Proverbs 11:24,25

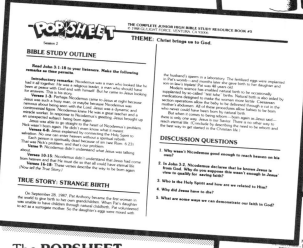

POPSHEET

Session 2

THEME: Christ brings us to God.

BIBLE STUDY OUTLINE

Read John 3:1-18 to your listeners. Make the following remarks as time permits.

Introductory remarks: Nicodemus was a man who looked like he had it all together. He was a religious leader, a man who should have been at peace with God and with himself. But he came to Jesus looking for answers. This is his story.

Verse 1-3: Perhaps Nicodemus came to Jesus at night because Jesus was such a busy man, or maybe because Nicodemus was nervous about being seen with the Lord. Jesus was a dynamic and controversial figure. Nicodemus knew He was a great teacher and a miracle worker. In response to Nicodemus's greeting, Jesus brought up an unexpected subject: being born again.

Jesus was able to go straight to the heart of Nicodemus's problem. Nick wasn't born again. He didn't even know what it meant.

Verses 4-8: Jesus explained by connecting the Holy Spirit to salvation. No one can enter heaven without a spiritual rebirth. Each person is spiritually dead because of sin (see Rom. 6:23). That was Nick's problem, and that's our problem.

Verse 9: Nicodemus didn't understand what Jesus was talking about.

Verses 10-15: Nicodemus didn't understand that Jesus had come from heaven and that He must die so that all could have eternal life.

Verses 16-18: These verses describe the way to be born again. (Now tell the True Story.)

the husband's sperm in a laboratory. The fertilized eggs were implanted in Pat's womb—and months later she gave birth to her daughter and son-in-law's triplets! Pat was 48 years old.

Modern science has enabled natural birth to be occasionally supplanted by so-called "test tube" births. Natural birth is also aided by medications designed to make the woman more fertile. Cesarean section operations allow the baby to be delivered through a cut in the mother's abdomen. All of these procedures allow babies to be born who never could have been born by natural birth.

But when it comes to being reborn—born again as Jesus said—there is only one way. Jesus is our Savior. There is no other way to reach eternal life. (Conclude by describing the need to be reborn and the best way to get started in the Christian life.)

DISCUSSION QUESTIONS

1. Why wasn't Nicodemus good enough to reach heaven on his own?

2. In John 3:2, Nicodemus declares that he knows Jesus is from God. Why do you suppose this wasn't enough in Jesus' view to qualify for saving faith?

3. Who is the Holy Spirit and how are we related to Him?

4. Why did Jesus have to die?

5. What are some ways we can demonstrate our faith in God?

TRUE STORY: STRANGE BIRTH

On September 28, 1987, Pat Anthony became the first woman in the world to give birth to her own grandchildren. When Pat's daughter was unable to have children through natural childbirth, Pat volunteered to act as a surrogate mother. So the daughter's eggs were mixed with

The **POPSHEET** is a lecture-oriented version of the **Session Plan,** based on a different portion of the Scriptures. Use it as an alternative to the **Session Plan,** at another meeting later in the week, or combine it with the **Session Plan** as you see fit. **SEE PAGE 12.**

The **Popsheet** features **GAMES AND THINGS,** dozens of action games, special suggestions and ideas for your students to enjoy. **PAGE 14 CONTAINS DETAILS.**

MPLETE ... BIBLE STUDY RESOURCE BOOK #5

GAMES & THINGS

Action games.

DOGS

You're probably familiar with the old coordinated clap game—the leader rhythmically waves his or her arms in the air and each time the hands cross, the members of the audience must clap their hands. The leader may suddenly stop waving. Whoever claps is then out of the game.

This is a variation of that game. Whenever a player claps out of turn, he or she is not only eliminated from the game but also must get on all fours and bark like a dog for a few seconds. The next time someone is eliminated, he or she must bark—but so must all the players who were dogs before. Soon almost everyone will be barking. It's a riot.

TIGER BY THE TAIL

Players form a conga line—a single file line with each player placing his or her hands on the waist of the player ahead. The lead player has hands free; the object is for the lead player to catch the last player in the line. The last player tries to avoid capture. Anyone who breaks the line is eliminated. When the lead player catches the last player, the person behind the lead player becomes the new leader. This way everyone gets a chance to be the head and the tail of the tiger.

HITCH THE CABOOSE

This game requires at least eight players and a large amount of space. Players form conga lines of three or more people each. You need at least two lines, but the more the merrier. Two players remain free; they are not in any group (if you have a large number of lines, add a few more loose players).

At the signal, the conga lines run all over the area. The loose players try to attach themselves to the end of the lines. If a loose player captures a line, the first player in the line becomes a loose caboose.

The **CLIP ART AND OTHER GOODIES** section at the back of the book contains special art you can use to dress up your newsletters. **SEE PAGE 16 FOR COMPLETE INFORMATION.**

Session 8

FUN Page!

"Sleuth"

Toenail File: John 13:1-17

I was snooping—er, investigating the following incident.

LORD, ARE YOU GOING TO WASH MY FEET?

YOU DO NOT REALIZE NOW WHAT I AM DOING, BUT LATER YOU WILL UNDERSTAND.

DO YOU UNDERSTAND WHAT I HAVE DONE FOR YOU? YOU CALL ME TEACHER AND 'LORD,' AND RIGHTLY SO, FOR THAT IS WHAT I AM. NOW THAT I, YOUR LORD AND TEACHER, HAVE WASHED YOUR FEET, YOU ALSO SHOULD WASH ONE ANOTHER'S FEET. I HAVE SET YOU AN EXAMPLE THAT YOU SHOULD DO AS I HAVE DONE FOR YOU.

If I take off my shoes, maybe Jesus will wash my feet, too.

GASP!

Well, we live and learn. I learned to be careful with a nose as great as mine, and I learned that Jesus wants us to generously serve others.

One way to serve is by generously sharing with those who have less than we have. Think about this: if you share God's love with another, does that mean you end up with less love? If you share joy, does that mean you have less joy? When you give Jesus to another, do you no longer have Jesus yourself?

Share the riches God gives you. He'll make sure you never run dry!

175

BIBLE Study!

MONSTER BIBLE STUDY

BIBLE Study!

MONSTER BIBLE STUDY

BIBLE Study!

MONSTER BIBLE STUDY

THE SESSION PLANS

How to squeeze the most out of each Bible study.

Every Session Plan contains the following features:

1. INTRODUCTORY INFORMATION

WHAT THE SESSION IS ABOUT states the main thrust of the lesson.

Your students will examine all verses listed in **SCRIPTURE STUDIED.**

The **KEY PASSAGE** is also the memory verse given on the **Gateway** student worksheet and the **Fun Page** take-home paper.

AIMS OF THE SESSION are what you hope to achieve during class time. You may wish to privately review these after class as a measure of your success.

Wise Living

SESSION 6

WHAT THE SESSION IS ABOUT
We need God's wisdom in order to make the right decisions in life.

SCRIPTURE STUDIED
Psalm 14:1; Proverbs 1:7; 2:6,7; 3:5,6; 14:9; 16:7; 19:8; 29:9,11; Matthew 7:24-29; Romans 1:21,22; 1 Corinthians 10:12; Galatians 6:3; Titus 3:3; James 1:5; 3:13-18.

KEY PASSAGE
"If any of you lacks wisdom, he should ask God, who gives generously to all without finding fault, and it will be given to him." James 1:5

AIMS OF THE SESSION
During this session your learners will:
1. Describe from Scripture the contrasts between a fool and a wise person;
2. Discuss the differences that God's wisdom can make in a person's life;
3. Select a specific area about which to ask God for wisdom.

INSIGHTS FOR THE LEADER

If confusion about who they are, what values they should hold, and what feelings they should experience is the ailment of typical junior highers, then the wisdom to do the right thing is the needed cure. Unfortunately, it is noticeably lacking in the lives of most people.

Wisdom is not a very popular commodity in the youth world. It is confused with visions of craggy, white-haired old men sitting in brooding silence and occasionally proclaiming a great insight (for those who have the patience to sit around long enough to hear). Wisdom is equated with age and experience and does not appear to kids to be attractive or particularly desirable.

The truth of the matter is that wisdom is what all people need, no matter what their age. It is the focal point of maturity and the anchor for good thinking, the anchor in the swirling current of modern thought.

Your students face the struggle...

and everyday, involving the ability to understand God's truth and apply it to daily life. It is often vividly contrasted in Scripture with its opposite—foolishness.

The biblical picture indicates that everyone is moving toward becoming wise or becoming foolish. There does not appear to be much middle ground. Scripture tells us that true wisdom comes only from God (see Prov. 1:7; 2:6,7) and that it is directly related to how we obey His Word. Proverbs 3:5,6 says, "Lean not on your own understanding; in all your ways acknowledge him, and he will make your paths straight."

In stark contrast, The Bible states, "The fool says in his heart, 'There is no God'" (Ps. ...

2. INSIGHTS FOR THE LEADER

This part of each lesson is background for you, the leader. Study this section with your Bible open and watch for useful information and insights which will further equip you to lead the class session.

Things to note about the Session Plan:

The **Session Plan** makes heavy use of **Bible Learning Activities**. A Bible Learning Activity (BLA) is precisely what it sounds like—an activity students perform to learn about the Bible. Because action is employed, the student has a much greater chance of **comprehending** and **retaining** spiritual insights. And because you, the leader, can see what the student is doing—whether it's a written assignment, skit or art activity—you can readily **measure** the student's comprehension. The BLA allows you to **walk about the classroom** as students work, answering questions or dealing with problem students. Furthermore, it's **easier to teach well** using BLAs. If you've never used BLAs before, you will quickly find them much simpler to prepare and deliver than a whole session of lecture.

The **Session Plan** provides guided conversation—suggestions on what to say throughout the class time. Notice that the guided conversation is always printed in **bold type** in the **Session Plan**. Regular light type indicates instructions to you, the teacher.

3. SESSION PLAN

This heading introduces the step-by-step lesson plan. With careful planning, you can easily tailor each session to the amount of class time you have.

4. BEFORE CLASS BEGINS

This is a convenient list of any special preparation or materials required.

5. ATTENTION GRABBER

Who knows what lurks in the minds of your students as they file into your room? The **Attention Grabber** will stimulate their interest and focus their thinking on the theme of the lesson.

The **Attention Grabber,** as well as other parts of the **Session Plan,** often—but not always—contain an additional alternate activity. These alternates are identified by the titles **CREATIVE OPTION, OPTIONAL** or similar designations. Choose the activity that best suits the needs of your class and fits your time schedule.

6. BIBLE EXPLORATION

The **Bible Exploration** is the heart of your class session because it involves each learner directly in the study of God's Word. It is during this period that you will invite the students to explore and discover **what the Bible says and means** and to discuss **how it applies to each student.**

SESSION PLAN

BEFORE CLASS BEGINS: Photocopy the Gateway and Fun Page.

Attention Grabber

ATTENTION GRABBER (3-5 minutes)

Ask students, **What do you think a "loser" looks like?** As they respond, write their comments on the chalkboard. (Most of their responses will be physical descriptions.)

Then ask, **What do you think a fool looks like?** Again record their answers. Then ask: **In your opinion, what is the difference between a loser and a fool? What would be the opposite of a fool?**

Make a transition by saying something like this:

You can't tell who's a fool just by look[ing] fool might be the best-looking person if we look only at the surface. So we h[ave] look a bit deeper. Today we are going a look at what it is to be truly wise an[d] it is to be a fool. I'm going to assume nobody wants to become a fool. But m[aybe] us have a lot to learn about becoming That learning process can begin—or continue—today.

Bible Exploration

EXPLORATION (20-35 minutes)

Step 1 (10-15 minutes): Have students form at least two groups of up to four per group. Direct attention to the "Describe-a-Fool/Words of Wisdom" sections of the Gateway. Assign half the groups to work on "Describe-a-Fool" while the rest do "Words of Wisdom." Tell class, **Work together in your groups to look up the Scriptures and label the drawings according to the information you find.**

Step 2 (5-10 minutes): Regain the at[tention of] the class and ask groups to report their fi[ndings on] three or four of the questions you select. [Add] any additional insights needed using ma[terial in] INSIGHTS FOR THE LEADER.

Step 3 (5-7 minutes): Lead a class d[iscussion] based on the following four questions. [Provide] added insights as needed using materia[l in] INSIGHTS FOR THE LEADER.

---

7. CONCLUSION AND DECISION

Each **Session Plan** provides this opportunity for students to deal with the questions, **What does the Bible mean to me? How can I put what I just learned into practice in my own life?** Be sure to leave enough time at the end of each session for the **Conclusion and Decision** activity.

8. NOTES

Every page of the **Session Plan** allows space for you to jot notes as you prepare for class. Also, you will find **important reminders** and **suggestions** listed in **bold type** to catch your attention.

NECESSARY CLASSROOM SUPPLIES

The Session Plan Bible study activities require that you make the following items readily available to students:

• A Bible for each student (Essential!) • Paper and pencils or pens • Felt markers • Butcher paper for posters • Transparent tape • Scissors

You will need a chalkboard and chalk, or overhead projector, transparencies and transparency markers.

Special requirements will be listed in the proper **Session Plans.**

THE GATEWAY
STUDENT WORKSHEETS

The **Gateway** helps students enter into the reality of God's truth.

The page immediately following each **Session Plan** is the **Gateway** worksheet for your students. Here's how to use the **Gateway**:

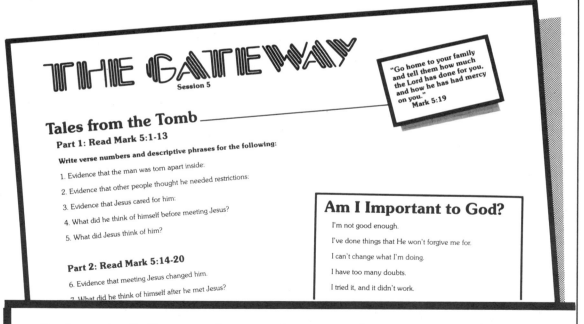

THE GATEWAY
Session 5

"Go home to your family and tell them how much the Lord has done for you, and how he has had mercy on you."
Mark 5:19

Tales from the Tomb
Part 1: Read Mark 5:1-13
Write verse numbers and descriptive phrases for the following:

1. Evidence that the man was torn apart inside:

2. Evidence that other people thought he needed restrictions:

3. Evidence that Jesus cared for him:

4. What did he think of himself before meeting Jesus?

5. What did Jesus think of him?

Part 2: Read Mark 5:14-20

6. Evidence that meeting Jesus changed him.

7. What did he think of himself after he met Jesus?

Am I Important to God?

I'm not good enough.

I've done things that He won't forgive me for.

I can't change what I'm doing.

I have too many doubts.

I tried it, and it didn't work.

Each session's **Gateway** features that session's memory verse (which is also printed on the **Fun Page** take-home paper). If you have a little extra time at the end of the lesson, review the memory verse with your students.

1. Before class, use your church photocopier to reproduce enough student worksheets for your learners and a few extra for visitors. There is never more than one **Gateway** worksheet per session—some sessions have none at all.

2. The **Gateways** are generally used throughout each **Session Plan**. The best time to distribute them to students is when the **Session Plan** first calls for their use. Always keep a copy for yourself.

3. Be sure to have plenty of blank paper for students' written assignments—the **Gateways** don't have much extra space.

4. It may help to have your students fold their **Gateway** into their Bibles if there is a gap between usage of the worksheet. This will aid you in avoiding the dreaded Paper Airplane Syndrome!

5. Collect and save the worksheets once every few weeks. (Do not collect worksheets that contain private confessions to God or the like.) You can follow the progress of your students by examining their work. Parents, too, will want to see what their kids are learning.

THE TEACHING RESOURCE
PAGES

Special goodies
to help you teach.

A few sessions require extra goodies such as board games or scrambled Bible verses. These are provided by the **Teaching Resource Pages** which follow the **Gateway** student worksheet in the appropriate sessions.

The **Session Plans** and the **Teaching Resource Pages** contain complete instructions.

I Do

Answer the questions below honestly.

I study: ☐ constantly ☐ seldom

I pray: ☐ when I'm in trouble ☐ seldom ☐ often

I don't mind if I wear out-of-date clothes: ☐ true ☐ false

I watch TV for about _____ hours per day.

What I love most of all is:

The last time I said, "Thanks" to my folks was:

I read God's Word: ☐ often ☐ seldom

I feel I should change _____ before God will
let me go to heaven.

Belief Quiz

	I believe it!	I don't believe it!
1. Good grades are very important to get.	_____	_____
2. God hears and answers my prayers.	_____	_____
3. Being accepted at school is vital.	_____	_____
4. My time belongs to God.	_____	_____
5. Christ is first in my life.	_____	_____
6. It is important to show gratitude.	_____	_____
7. The Bible is a dependable guide for my life.	_____	_____
8. I believe Jesus Christ died for all my sins.	_____	_____

THE FUN PAGE
TAKE-HOME PAPERS

Give your students a treat! The new, expanded Fun Page combines games, cartoons, short stories, interviews, memory verses and daily devotional studies into an enjoyable, fun-filled take-home paper.

Features:

Each **Fun Page** contains a comic strip, short story or interview designed to amplify the insights gained in the classroom. The comic strip is called **The Sleuth.** It centers on the adventures of a snoopy detective who investigates the truths your students have been studying in the Bible.

Sharing things with others is a good habit. It's a good way to win friends, that's for sure. Luke 6:38 gives an important tip regarding our generosity. You can find out what Luke 6:38 says by looking it up in the Bible—but that would be too easy! Do it the hard way: unscramble the words below (the ones in bold type) to correctly spell out what Jesus said.

"**VEIG**, AND IT **LIWL** BE **EIGNV** TO YOU. A **DOGO SEREMAU**, **DSSEERP WOND**, **AENKHS RHETTEOG** AND **GNUNINR EVRO**, **ILWL** BE **DPOEUR TOIN OUYR ALP**. **RFO TWHI** THE **UAMEERS UYO EUS**, IT WILL BE **AUMESEDR OT UYO**."

DAILY NUGGETS

Day 1 Read Acts 20:35. What could you give to another this week?

Day 2 Ephesians 5:2. What does this verse say that Christ has given for us?

Day 3 Luke 16:19-31. What could the rich man have done for Lazarus? What did the rich man want Lazarus to do for him?

Day 4 John 13:14,15. What is the meaning of the example Christ provided?

Day 5 1 John 2:10. How could a Christian cause another person to stumble or trip up in his or her spiritual life?

Day 6 1 Corinthians 10:24. Whose good should we seek?

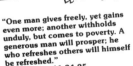

"One man gives freely, yet gains even more; another withholds unduly, but comes to poverty. A generous man will prosper; he who refreshes others will himself be refreshed."
Proverbs 11:24,25

On the back of the **Fun Page** you'll find Bible games that your students will love: mazes, crosswords, word searches—games ranging from the simple to the extremely challenging. Again, they are designed to reinforce what the students have learned during the session time.

The **Daily Nuggets** section is a simple six-day devotional based on passages related to the Scriptures studied in class.

The **Hot Thot** memory verse helps students lock the wisdom of God's Word into their minds and hearts.

How to Use the Fun Page:

Photocopy both sides of the **Fun Page** back-to-back, just as it appears in this manual. (If your copy machine cannot do this, we suggest you copy each side on a separate sheet.) Make enough copies for your students plus a few extras for visitors. Note: You may like to occasionally save the **Fun Page** game for use during another Bible study time.

You can use the Fun Page several ways:

As a **take-home paper** to extend the classroom into the week. Hand out copies as students leave class.

As a special **Bible Learning Activity** during class. (Some of the games would make interesting **Attention Grabbers,** for example.)

Make it the **focal point of another Bible study.** For instance, if you used the **Session Plan** Sunday morning, you could reinforce the lesson during an informal midweek meeting by involving students in answering the questions in the **Daily Nuggets** section.

Even absentees can be involved. Put the **Fun Page** into an envelope along with a personal note to that learner who needs a little encouragement.

THE POPSHEET
LECTURE BIBLE STUDIES

"Pop" these Popsheets out of this book and give them to the leader of your youth group's other meetings. Great for an at-home Bible study, a camp retreat, games night or special event.

Youth groups come in all sizes and shapes. So do youth programs. Meetings vary widely in style—ranging from Sunday morning Bible studies with singing and announcements, to deeper discipleship programs for motivated students, to the fun and action of game nights with very short Bible messages.

The **Popsheets** offer a good source of creative thinking for whatever type of program you have. **Popsheets** are packed with Bible stories, object lessons, case studies, discussion questions and fast-paced games and other ideas aimed at the junior high "squirrel" mentality! Each **Popsheet** covers the same basic theme as the accompanying **Session Plan,** but the stories, verses, object lessons and case studies are all new and fresh.

The advantages?

● For students who attended the **Session Plan** class, a fresh new perspective on the topic. A great way to insure retention.

● For learners who missed the **Session Plan** class, a good way to keep current with the other students. This is a sound method to guarantee that all your youth group members explore every topic in a Bible study series.

● Or use your creativity to replace some of the Bible Learning Activities in the **Session Plans** with object lessons and short stories from the **Popsheets.**

THEME

Roughly the same theme as the accompanying **Session Plan.**

BIBLE STUDY OUTLINE

A suggested Bible passage with a list of important points to make during your lecture, the **Bible Study Outline** offers a *basic* lesson plan to stimulate your thinking as you prayerfully prepare your message. **Use your own creativity and ability to "flesh it out."** There is plenty here to help you create outstanding Bible messages your students will enjoy and remember.

Notice that the **Bible Study Outline** contains no **Bible Learning Activities.** The **Popsheet** is designed to be a short Bible message (five to ten minutes) that you can give at an informal games night, camp cabin devotional, or similar setting.

OBJECT LESSON

Each **Popsheet** has an object lesson, short story or case study. (A case study is a description of an event or situation a junior high student is likely to face in life.) These add spice to your messages. A good object lesson, for instance, and the spiritual truth it conveys, can be remembered for a lifetime.

THE COMPLETE JUNIOR HIGH BIBLE STUDY RESOURCE BOOK #5
© 1988 GL/LIGHT FORCE, VENTURA, CA 93006

THEME: Christ brings us to God.

Session 2

BIBLE STUDY OUTLINE

Read John 3:1-18 to your listeners. Make the following remarks as time permits.

Introductory remarks: Nicodemus was a man who looked like he had it all together. He was a religious leader, a man who should have been at peace with God and with himself. But he came to Jesus looking for answers. This is his story.

Verses 1-3: Perhaps Nicodemus came to Jesus at night because Jesus was such a busy man, or maybe because Nicodemus was nervous about being seen with the Lord. Jesus was a dynamic and controversial figure. Nicodemus knew He was a great teacher and a miracle worker. In response to Nicodemus's greeting, Jesus brought up an unexpected subject: being born again.

Jesus was able to go straight to the heart of Nicodemus's problem. Nick wasn't born again. He didn't even know what it meant.

Verses 4-8: Jesus explained by connecting the Holy Spirit to salvation. No one can enter heaven without a spiritual rebirth.

Each person is spiritually dead because of sin (see Rom. 6:23). That was Nick's problem, and that's our problem.

Verse 9: Nicodemus didn't understand what Jesus was talking about.

Verses 10-15: Nicodemus didn't understand that Jesus had come from heaven and that He must die so that all could have eternal life.

Verses 16-18: These verses describe the way to be born again. *(Now tell the True Story.)*

TRUE STORY: STRANGE BIRTH

On September 28, 1987, Pat Anthony became the first woman in the world to give birth to her own grandchildren. When Pat's daughter was unable to have children through natural childbirth, Pat volunteered to act as a surrogate mother. So the daughter's eggs were mixed with the husband's sperm in a laboratory. The fertilized eggs were implanted in Pat's womb—and months later she gave birth to her daughter and son-in-law's triplets! Pat was 48 years old.

Modern science has enabled natural birth to be occasionally supplanted by so-called "test tube" births. Natural birth is also aided by medications designed to make the woman more fertile. Caesarean section operations allow the baby to be delivered through a cut in the mother's abdomen. All of these procedures allow babies to be born who never could have been born by natural birth.

But when it comes to being reborn—born again as Jesus said— there is only one way. Jesus is our Savior. There is no other way to reach eternal life. (Conclude by describing the need to be reborn and the best way to get started in the Christian life.)

DISCUSSION QUESTIONS

1. Why wasn't Nicodemus good enough to reach heaven on his own?

2. In John 3:2, Nicodemus declares that he knows Jesus is from God. Why do you suppose this wasn't enough in Jesus' view to qualify for saving faith?

3. Who is the Holy Spirit and how are we related to Him?

4. Why did Jesus have to die?

5. What are some ways we can demonstrate our faith in God?

DISCUSSION QUESTIONS

You may wish to involve your students in your lectures by asking them about the issues and implications of the Bible study. Feel free to modify or add to the questions to more nearly suit your students' needs.

The **Popsheet** is intended to be folded and placed in a Bible for easy reference as the leader teaches.

GAMES AND THINGS

THE COMPLETE
JUNIOR HIGH BIBLE STUDY
RESOURCE BOOK #5

Action games.

__DOGS__

You're probably familiar with the old coordinated clap game—the leader rhythmically waves his or her arms in the air and each time the hands cross, the members of the audience must clap their hands. The leader may suddenly stop waving; whoever claps is then out of the game.

This is a variation of that game. Whenever a player claps out of turn, he or she is not only eliminated from the game but also must get on all fours and bark like a dog for a few seconds. The next time someone is eliminated, he or she must bark—but so must all the players who were dogs before. Soon almost everyone will be barking. It's a riot.

TIGER BY THE TAIL

Players form a conga line—a single file line with each player placing his or her hands on the waist of the player ahead. The lead player has hands free; the object is for the lead player to catch the last player in the line. The last player tries to avoid capture. Anyone who breaks the line is eliminated. When the lead player catches the last player, the person behind the lead player becomes the new leader. This way, everyone gets a chance to be the head and the tail of the tiger.

HITCH THE CABOOSE

This game requires at least eight players and a large amount of space. Players form conga lines of three or more people each. You need at least two lines, but the more the merrier. Two players remain free; they are not in any group (if you have a large number of lines, add a few more loose players).

At the signal, the conga lines run all over the area. The loose players try to attach themselves to the end of the lines. If a loose player captures a line, the first player in the line becomes a loose caboose.

On the reverse side of the **Popsheet** you will find **Games and Things,** a wonderful collection of:

1. Action activities for your games night, youth group parties, church socials, youth Vacation Bible Schools, camps—wherever kids are gathered. Give a copy to the leader of the games night program; he or she will love you for it!

2. Creative suggestions for social events, community involvement and the like.

3. Paper games similar to the **Fun Page** games—Use them as the focal point of an at-home style Bible study for a nice change of pace.

4. Special ideas such as posters (which you can enlarge on a copy machine or opaque projector). These special ideas will appear occasionally in this and future **Junior High Bible Study Resource Books.**

EXCITING OPTIONS FOR THE SMALL YOUTH PROGRAM

Mix and match: Putting together a customized class time tailored to *your* students.

We hope that by reading these introductory pages you've come to realize how hard we are working to bring you a truly useful resource manual for your youth program. There is plenty here for your Sunday School classes, midweek Bible studies, games meetings and special events—even if you do all these things every week.

But what do you do with all these ideas if you're a small church with no youth staff (or one poor overworked "volunteer")? This is where **The Complete Junior High Bible Study Resource Book** really shines. By spending a few hours each week in preparation, you can mix and match the best features of each **Session Plan, Gateway, Fun Page, Popsheet** and **Games and Things** to build a wonderful classroom experience for your students. This illustration gives you some idea of the scope available to you:

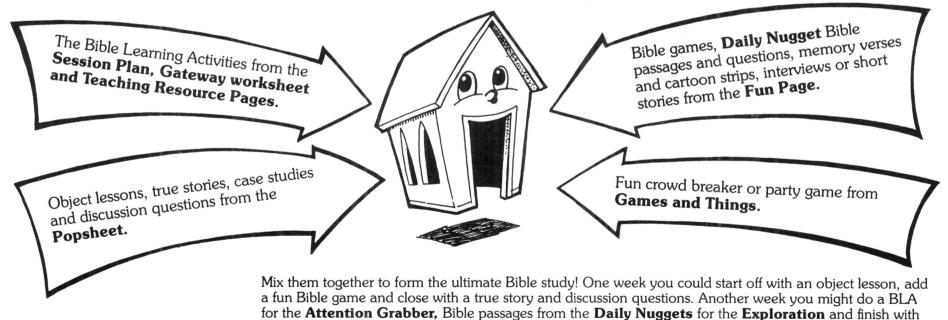

The Bible Learning Activities from the **Session Plan, Gateway worksheet and Teaching Resource Pages**.

Bible games, **Daily Nugget** Bible passages and questions, memory verses and cartoon strips, interviews or short stories from the **Fun Page**.

Object lessons, true stories, case studies and discussion questions from the **Popsheet**.

Fun crowd breaker or party game from **Games and Things**.

Mix them together to form the ultimate Bible study! One week you could start off with an object lesson, add a fun Bible game and close with a true story and discussion questions. Another week you might do a BLA for the **Attention Grabber**, Bible passages from the **Daily Nuggets** for the **Exploration** and finish with a fun party game to celebrate God's provision. Each week can be a new and exciting experience that your students will look forward to.

INTRODUCTION TO CLIP ART

Good news for those who can't draw.

If you want your class or youth group to increase in size—and who doesn't— you'll welcome the **Clip Art and Other Goodies** section found at the rear of this book. Create your own terrific monthly youth group activity calendars, announcement sheets and posters. It's fun and easy! Simply follow the tips and techniques in the **Clip Art and Other Goodies** section; you'll produce great "promo pieces" that will attract kids to your Bible studies and other events.

Remember: Even if you can't draw cartoons, with the right promotional clip art you can draw kids!

God Loves Us SESSION 1

WHAT THE SESSION IS ABOUT

God made us, and He loves and understands His creation.

SCRIPTURE STUDIED

Psalm 139

KEY PASSAGE

"I praise you because I am fearfully and wonderfully made; your works are wonderful, I know that full well." Psalm 139:14

AIMS OF THE SESSION

During this session your learners will:

1. Search for evidence of God's love in a Bible passage about His making of a human being;
2. Identify ways people might respond upon learning of God's attitude toward them;
3. Write a prayer using Psalm 139:23,24 as a guide.

INSIGHTS FOR THE LEADER

Junior highers have trouble liking and being at ease with themselves. They are often physically awkward and verbally uncertain. They have lost their secure identity as children, but they aren't treated as adults—and they may not even qualify yet as "youth" (those wise, experienced high schoolers).

Given all this uncertainty about who they are, junior highers may not get much immediate comfort from being told "God made you." Their reaction may be, "So why did God bother?"

Special Creation

The Scripture for this session is a psalm about God's making of a human being: not the original creation of mankind, but one person's meditation on how carefully God made him and how well God knows him. It could be anyone's account of how he or she received life from God. The students will search the psalm for evidence of God's love in His work of making this human being, and any human being, including themselves.

Psalm 139 begins with the writer's sense of the Lord's complete knowledge of his person (vv. 1-12). Nothing is hidden from the Lord's wisdom: "O Lord, you have searched me and you know me . . . . Before a word is on my tongue you know it completely, O Lord" (vv. 1,4). No one can escape from God: "Where can I go from your Spirit? Where can I flee from your presence?" (v. 7).

To a junior high student, such total divine knowledge can sound intimidating, like an "All-seeing Eye" that follows him or her everywhere. Notice, however, that the psalmist does not react to God's omniscience with timidity or cowering, but rather with joy and awe. "Such knowledge is too wonderful for me, too lofty for me to attain . . . . How precious to me are your thoughts, O God!" (vv. 6,17).

The reason God so intimately knows the writer of the psalm—and us—is that He made each of us. He not only created man and woman "in the beginning" as recorded in Genesis; He also plans and makes each individual who comes into the world. The psalmist describes that process poetically in verses 13 through 16. "You knit me together in my mother's womb" (Psa. 139:13).

Some of your students may have been told by their parents that they were "accidents." On top of all their general confusion about just being alive, the knowledge that they were unplanned (and therefore, they feel, unwanted) may be unbearable. Be sensitive to the probability that some of your students feel they are not even supposed to be here in the first place. If you had the same experience, your students should hear you talk about it during this session. How did you feel about yourself and about God when you found out? How has God taught you that He had a reason

for your being born? And how have you found a purpose for your life?

To your students, physical attractiveness is very important and desirable (and, some think, unattainable). Psalm 139 can challenge their standard of "good-looking = likeable" by showing them that God carefully creates every person, no matter how he or she measures up to the latest blue jean or cosmetic ad.

Special People

As you talk about the biblical truth that all people are planned and made by God, students may ask the logical question, "Why does God make people with birth defects? Does He really deliberately plan for some people to be born blind, mentally retarded, unable to walk?" You might mention that the Bible says all of creation is flawed because of sin (see Rom. 8:19-22; Gen. 3:17,18). Because of the Fall, the spiritual and physical nature of the human race has been deteriorating. Illnesses have crept into it. Genetic difficulties have arisen. Environmental pollutants affect people adversely. God does not automatically reverse these problems for His people. He renews us now in our relationship with Christ, but He will perfect us spiritually and physically when we come into our eternal state.

None of this, however, provides a complete and satisfactory answer to the question we have posed. There are some questions for which the final answer cannot be found in this life. Our human understanding is too shallow, and God's thoughts are too deep for us to be able to understand Him fully or to grasp the reason for everything He does.

Some things we do know, however. God has assured us of His love in the Scripture; He has demonstrated it in His Son. He has assured us that, if we love Him and are called according to His purpose, all things will work together for our good and will make us more Christlike (see Rom. 8:28,29). He also assures us that the various trials we encounter in life will lead to the development of Christian character (see Rom. 5:3-5; Jas. 1:2-4). We do not know just why God allows disabilities. We do not understand how He could actually plan for them and be consistent with His love. But it boils down to this: There are disabled people among us. We need to love them with God's love and encourage them with His comfort.

Psalm 139 has to do with more than the fact that God has engineered us. A cabinetmaker could produce "just another bookcase" and feel no emotion about it. But God's making of us is more than a display of technical skill. He made us in His image, able to respond to and reflect His loving nature. Clues to God's love for the individual are evident throughout Psalm 139.

Wickedness

All of the psalm will be studied—even verses 19-22. After studying verses 1-18, explain that the author knows that God made and loves all people; therefore, He wants goodness, not wickedness, to come out on top. It is natural, as people come closer to God, that they are more and more repulsed by evil. Sometimes people feel a need to defend God (as if He weren't big enough to take care of Himself). The psalmist's revulsion against God-haters is natural and even appropriate. The danger lies in being unable to separate the person from the actions.

The psalmist realized the need to watch out for evil in himself and to receive God's cleansing. "Search me, O God, and know my heart; See if there is any offensive way in me" (vv. 23,24).

Knowing that God made them and loves them invites response from learners. Do their lives honor or dishonor their Creator? Your students will write a prayer based on the last two verses of the psalm—confessing some way they have not been all that God intended, and showing their intentions to follow Him.

SESSION PLAN

BEFORE CLASS BEGINS: Now's a good time to make sure your classroom has all the items listed under "Necessary Classroom Supplies" on page 7. If you happen to be teaching a new group of students, you may wish to distribute copies of "The Mug File" questionnaire (see the "Clip Art and Other Goodies" section on page 171). Allow your students to complete the questionnaire at the beginning or the end of the class time. See *Step 2* of the ATTENTION GRABBER for special preparation. Photocopy the Fun Page take-home papers. There are no Gateway worksheets or Teaching Resource pages for this session.

Attention Grabber

ATTENTION GRABBER (3-5 minutes)

Step 1 (2-3 minutes): Distribute paper and pencils. Tell students, **I want you each to draw a simple picture of yourself. It can be silly, it can be a lousy drawing—it doesn't matter. Just make it unique because you are unique.**

Collect the drawings and mix them in a pile at the front of the room.

Step 2 (1-2 minutes): Now ask students to come forward and take their drawings. By previous arrangement with you, one student will deliberately take the *wrong* drawing—one he or she did not make. (You can talk to the student just before class

time.) Someone will then be left with an unfamiliar creation and will complain that it isn't the one he or she made.

Confess that the task was rigged and have your accomplice give the drawing back to the rightful person.

Make a transition to the Bible Exploration by saying something like, **It was easy for each of you to recognize and pick your own drawing. God made each one of us and He, too, knows each one of us intimately and cares for us individually.**

Bible Exploration

EXPLORATION (25-35 minutes)

Step 1 (1-2 minutes): Have students form groups of three to four. Then say, **First, let's read Psalm**

139. Give students time to find the psalm.

Have someone who is a strong reader read

NOTES

verses 1-12 aloud, or you read it aloud while the learners follow in their Bibles.

Step 2 (3-5 minutes): After the reading, ask **What's this section of the psalm all about?** Learners may give several different answers expressing God's knowledge of us. Write this idea on the chalkboard: "God knows me."

Repeat this process with verses 13-18. Learners should identify God's creation as the focus of this section. Write "God made me" on the chalkboard.

Tell the learners, **There's a third thing this psalm is about, which we'll read and study in a moment.** Write "God loves me" on the board.

Step 3 (10-12 minutes): Explain, **God's love for us runs throughout this psalm. There are lots of clues here about His attitude toward us and how important we are to Him. Work together in your groups to find the clues to God's love, care, watchfulness and knowledge of you. As you read each verse, 1 through 18, discuss what it tells you about God's love for you. Write down what you discover in each verse.** Write "God's love, care, watchfulness and knowledge of you" on the chalkboard.

If a group appears to be dashing through the passage with record speed, interrupt the members and ask for some sample answers for the first three verses. Are they thoughtful or unthinking? If they seem like quick guesses, encourage the learners to **Back up, slow down, and analyze what's going on in this statement. For instance, verse 1 says "O Lord, you have searched me and you know me." Do we bother to find out all about somebody, really get to know that person, if we aren't interested and don't care? God cares. He loves us and that's why He pays so much attention to us. The close attention He gives us is a clue that He cares, that He loves us. We don't have to break speed records. I won't give you an *F* if you don't get all the way through to verse 18!**

Let the groups resume work.

Step 4 (5-7 minutes): Ask a different group to share what they discovered for each verse. After each report ask if any group found anything

additional or different. If a group comes up with something you hadn't seen in the Scripture, be sure to say so! Affirm them for their insight. When the class digs deeper than the teacher, you are getting somewhere in making mature disciples.

Step 5 (1-5 minutes): When all the clues of God's love in Psalm 139:1-18 have been reported, say something like this: **God loves what He has made—us—just because He made us. In fact, the reason He made us is that He loves us. He doesn't love us if we're beautiful or smart— He just loves us. Sometimes we wonder why God made us like He did—or even why He made us at all! We look at each other and we imagine God did a better job on Mr. Gorgeous and Miss Vogue Cover than He did on Miss Frumpy and Mr. Zero. But the Bible says, "The Lord does not look at the things man looks at. Man looks at the outward appearance, but the Lord looks at the heart"** (1 Sam. 16:7).

(If you have had the experience of being told you were unwanted, or if you know someone who had to cope with that situation, this would be a good time to tell the story.)

Step 6 (2-3 minutes): **As you were reading through the entire psalm, you probably noticed that change of mood toward the end. All of a sudden the writer starts talking about how God should do away with wicked people.**

Have someone read verses 19-22. Ask, **Why do you think that is in this psalm?** Allow students time to respond.

Knowing about God's love makes us stand up against unloving people. But it's very easy to become unloving while we're standing up for love! Note that after his outburst, the writer immediately asked God to examine him. (Read vv. 23,24.) **Seeing how much God loves us has that effect on us. We realize how we've failed Him, and how He loves us anyway. We want Him to lovingly change us into people who follow Him more closely.**

Step 7 (2 minutes): Work together with the entire class to brainstorm ways people might respond on hearing about God's attitude toward them in Psalm 139. Summarize their ideas on the chalkboard. Point out that knowing God loves each of us gives us a reason to have a positive outlook and to be filled with joy.

Conclusion and Decision

CONCLUSION (5-7 minutes)

Say something like this: **The writer of this psalm knew that God loved him, and he resented the fact that some people were unloving and mean. But then he looked at himself and he knew he wasn't perfect either. That's the effect that Psalm 139 should have on us. As God searches and knows our hearts, He shows us where we're falling short and where we're going our own way, away from Him.**

Read verses 23 and 24 aloud, or have a student read them.

Has God been showing you lately where you're unloving, or stubborn, or selfish? He loves you, and because He loves you, He wants you to go the right way. And for every "don't" God tells you about, He also tells you a "do." For every "stop" there's a "start"! What can you do to begin following the way He shows you today, and tomorrow, and this week?

Have each person write a simple prayer to God. These will not be shared aloud unless someone is willing to do so. You will set a good example of an adult trying to grow in the Lord if you write and share a prayer.

Pray aloud for yourself and your students, thanking God that He loves you and each of them, asking Him to help you live closer to Him this week.

Distribute the Fun Page take-home paper as students leave.

ALTERNATE CONCLUSION: (5-7 minutes)

Say something like this: **The writer of this psalm knew that God loved him, and he resented the fact that some people were unloving and mean. But then he looked at himself and he knew he wasn't perfect either. That's the effect that Psalm 139 should have on us. As God searches and knows our hearts, He shows us where we're falling short and where we're going our own way, away from Him.**

Read verses 23 and 24 aloud, or have a student read them.

Explain, **Rewrite Psalm 139:23,24 in your own words.**

You may wish to use the following as an example of what a student might write:

Look through me, God, and know all about my thoughts (how much I think about getting back at Mark for hurting me).

Test me and know how wrong it is for me to think that way.

See the bad attitude I have toward Mark, and help me to be his friend instead, because it's your way.

Close in prayer and distribute the Fun Page take-home paper.

Note: If you intend to use the CREATIVE ALTERNATE to the next session's ATTENTION GRABBER, you must prepare and mail letters to your students several days before class time. See the EXPLORATION for additional before class preparation (page 30).

21

Session 1

Hi there! I hope you enjoy this first issue of "The Sleuth" cartoon strip. The word *sleuth* means detective or investigator and that's just what we're going to do— investigate God's Word, the Bible. Oh, yeah— I'm the Sleuth, the little guy with the big nose.

Lame Excuses File

Current investigation: A look into some of the silly reasons people have for thinking God doesn't like them.

Silly Excuse #1

MY EARS STICK OUT—GOD MUST NOT LOVE ME!

Silly Excuse #2

I DIDN'T GET AN "A+" THIS TIME— I GUESS GOD DOESN'T LIKE ME!

Silly Excuse #3

I HAVE FEET LIKE BANANA BOATS—

GOD MUST NOT LOVE ME!

Silly Excuse #4

MY PARENTS ARE FIGHTING— GOD PROBABLY BLAMES ME!

BUT, IT'S NOT YOUR FAULT!

This all seemed pretty silly to me. I decided to find Jesus and see what He had to say about it.

FOR GOD SO LOVED THE WORLD THAT HE GAVE HIS ONE AND ONLY SON, THAT WHOEVER BELIEVES IN HIM SHALL NOT PERISH BUT HAVE ETERNAL LIFE. FOR GOD DID NOT SEND HIS SON INTO THE WORLD TO CONDEMN THE WORLD, BUT TO SAVE THE WORLD THROUGH HIM.

(JOHN 3:16,17)

Sleuth's comment: Jesus is never wrong! When He says God loves us, He's right!

No excuses.

Hot Text

"I praise you because I am fearfully and wonderfully made; your works are wonderful, I know that full well."
Psalm 139:14

GOD LOVES US! (Just the way we are.)

Sometimes we think that God must not like us much, because He made us with a big nose or lousy math skills. Sometimes we think God would like us more if we were smarter or better looking. Wrong!

This silly game pokes fun at this idea about God. Play it, it's fun. Here's how: Cut out the cards below. Shuffle them, then pick them one at a time to fill in the blanks on the 14 Lame Excuses. Use the first card you draw to fill in the blank of the first statement, the second card for the second statement, and so on. You'll end up with 14 pretty weird excuses! But even if they all made sense, they'd still be wrong. You see, God loves you just the way you are.

For an extra challenge—try to arrange the cards so that all the excuses seem to make sense (though they'll still be lame).

Lame Excuses
God doesn't like me because:

1. My ———— is ugly.

2. I've got too much ————.

3. I beat up on my ————.

4. My ———— is slow.

5. I don't get along with my ————.

6. I can't stand my ————.

7. I'm a total ————.

8. My ———— drains unexpectedly.

9. My ———— gets tied in knots.

10. I treat my best ———— like dirt.

11. I find it hard to keep a ————.

12. I'm foolish with my ————.

13. I'm lousy at telling a ————.

14. I guess I'm just a big ————.

FACE	FAT	KID BROTHER
BRAIN	MOTHER	TEACHER
KLUTZ	NOSE	TONGUE
FRIEND	SECRET	MONEY
JOKE	HAIRBALL	

DAILY NUGGETS
Wisdom from God's Word for you to read each day.

Day 1 Read Genesis 1:27,31; Revelation 4:11. In whose image did God create the human race? In light of these verses how do you think God feels about people? About you?

Day 2 John 10:14-16. How does the Good Shepherd show love for His sheep (v. 15)? What does the future hold for different groups under Christ's care?

Day 3 John 13:35. If Jesus says that loving one another shows that we are His disciples (followers), what does that tell us about God?

Day 4 John 14:23. How do we show our love for Jesus? How does Jesus respond to us when we love Him and demonstrate our love in the way He indicated?

Day 5 1 John 4:9,10. How has God shown love to us?

Day 6 Ephesians 5:1,2. What does Paul encourage Christians to do just as Christ did? Knowing that God loves you, list ways you could show His love to someone this week.

THE COMPLETE JUNIOR HIGH BIBLE STUDY RESOURCE BOOK #5
© 1988 GL/LIGHT FORCE, VENTURA, CA 93006

THEME: Because God made us, He understands us.

Session 1

BIBLE STUDY OUTLINE

Read the first chapter of Genesis aloud. Call your students' attention to God's creativity, and stress the several verses that mention God's satisfaction with what He created (e.g., "God saw that the light was good" in v. 4). Particularly note verse 31 in which God saw that all was very good. Emphasize the idea that since God made humanity, He obviously knows what makes each of us tick. He put us together and He can fix us when we are hurting or sad.

Do the Object Lesson demonstration.

OBJECT LESSON:

You need an object that represents a human being. A doll will do, or a stick figure constructed from Tinker Toys. Also, provide some mud, a bowl and towels for cleanup.

Show your listeners the doll or stick figure. Explain that it represents a typical human being—one who is in proper relationship with God and therefore spiritually A-OK. Drop the doll into the bowl of mud and stir it until filthy (you may wish to tear or cut the doll to pieces as you do this). Tell listeners that the doll now represents a human being who has become soiled and dirty by falling away from God. The mud represents sin; the disfiguring of the doll represents the spiritual (and oftentimes mental and physical) damage that sin does to a person. Be sure to point out that everybody has been messed up by sin.

Now ask your students if the doll can clean itself up and put itself back together. No, it needs your help. You can do it because you have the power and ability. In the same way, we cannot save ourselves from sin. Only God can do this, because He has the power and ability. He made us, as Genesis 1 points out, and therefore He knows exactly how to deal with our problems.

Wrap up the lesson by inviting anyone who feels a need for God's help to speak to Him in silent prayer and to talk to you after the meeting.

DISCUSSION QUESTIONS

1. In what ways are sin and dirt alike?

2. What sort of damage can sin do to a person?

3. In what ways does God deal with the problem of sin?

4. God made us. How does that help Him to understand us and sympathize with our problems?

5. Do you think God really cares about you as an individual and if so, why?

NOTES

Mystery guessing games.

These mystery guessing games will provide hours of challenge for a group of kids. You tell your listeners the end of a story and the kids have to guess the events that led to the ending. Participants ask questions, to which you can only answer yes, no, or "makes no difference" (the latter if the question has no bearing on the story). You can also repeat the end of the story if asked. You can drop hints if you want to wrap up the game in shorter time.

MOLLY LIES UNDER THE TROLLY

The end:

When they found her, Molly was lying on the tracks under the trolly car. There was no expression of pain on her face—she looked as if she was at peace. Molly did not die by accident or natural causes, yet she had neither committed suicide nor been murdered. What happened?

The solution:

Nothing happened. Molly wasn't dead—she was a trolly mechanic.

THE SEAL SHOW

Here's a silly one!

The end:

Everyday at the zoo, the trained seals gave three shows—one in the morning, one at noon and one in the afternoon. Today, the seals gave their morning show, took a break, then came back on stage for the second show. But they left the stage without performing and refused to come back. That afternoon, the seals gave their third show with no problems. Why wouldn't they do the noon show?

The solution:

The noon show's audience was made up entirely of nuns wearing black and white habits. The seals mistook the group for a killer whale and fled.

THE MAN IN THE DESERT

This one's pretty tough!

The end:

The dead man had been lying in the middle of the desert sands all summer, frozen solid. How was this possible?

The solution:

The man—an astronaut—was on Mars, where the summers are below zero.

Jesus Makes It Possible

WHAT THE SESSION IS ABOUT

Christ is the One who makes a relationship with God possible.

SCRIPTURE STUDIED

Ephesians 2:1-10

KEY PASSAGE

"For it is by grace you have been saved, through faith—and this not from yourselves, it is the gift of God—not by works, so that no one can boast." Ephesians 2:8,9

AIMS OF THE SESSION

During this session your learners will:

1. Examine how God through the ultimate gesture of love restored humanity's relationship with Him;
2. Write slogans about the relationship God wants to have with them;
3. Consider their personal relationship to Christ and their need to begin or renew that relationship.

INSIGHTS FOR THE LEADER

God created us as special people: as people who have worth and value, as people with whom He wants to have a relationship. Last week's session focused on this truth.

In this session you and your class are going to look at the barrier that stands in the way of the relationship that God wants to have with us, and at what He did to remove that obstacle in order to enable us to have that relationship.

Dead in Your Transgressions

Ephesians 2:1-10 is the Scripture for the session. Paul begins the passage by reminding the believers of how they used to live. Students who have been raised in the warm environment of a godly home and who have had great input from the Scripture may find it difficult to identify with the life-style Paul describes. Some young people even feel that they have missed something in their conversion experience if they didn't have to crawl out of the "pit of sin" or didn't get saved from something tangible and dramatic like drugs, crime or immorality.

Actually no one has to look very far to get a good dose of "the ways of the world" described by Paul. The apostle has not provided a list of specific sinful acts. He has instead put his finger on the root of all problems: willful disobedience against God caused by a sinful, selfish nature that seeks to satisfy its own desires. That old self-centered nature still clings to even the most devout saint. It is not necessary to go out and prove that you have it. A careful self-examination will reveal much more than we usually admit. It is this rebellion against God and His rule that shattered the connection between God and humanity, leaving people physically alive, but literally dead towards God and His benefits.

Sin has done more than just add some flaws to otherwise nice people. It has destroyed any capacity to win back a relationship with God. Dead men tell no tales, nor do they repair the damage that killed them. Therefore, humanity's only hope is for God to take action.

Alive with Christ

Paul says, "But because of his great love for us, God, who is rich in mercy, made us alive with Christ even when we were dead in transgressions" (Eph. 2:4,5). God wants a relationship with the people He created. Christ is the arm of God reaching out to reverse the damage caused by sin.

Although the passage does not speak specifically about Christ's sacrifice for our sin, there is obvious allusion to it. Your more mature Christians will quickly discern this.

The magnificence of Christ's work on our behalf dramatically emphasizes that there is nothing that we can do through our own efforts to earn this relationship with God. It is only by trust in and reliance on Jesus Christ

NOTES

that anyone comes to know the Creator. "For it is by grace [favor you don't deserve] you have been saved [rescued], through faith [trust, reliance on God]—and this not from yourselves, it is the gift of God—not by works [your own effort, goodness and striving], so that no one can boast (Eph. 2:8,9, with explanations). Just as God created people originally, with no human advice or assistance, so He now re-creates us "in Christ Jesus," by His grace and power. Good works can never create new life in the spiritually dead. But once we are alive in Christ, good works are the result God seeks, evidence that He has changed us from the self-centered, rebellious people we were before.

The passage clearly shows helpless humanity being rescued by a loving and caring God through a huge sacrifice on His part. Some of your students may have heard this many times, and the session will be a review for them. But perhaps there are several in your class who are new or who come from backgrounds where the gospel message is a strange language. Perhaps there are some who just recently have developed "ears to hear," and the truth that they have heard over and over again has finally sunk in. Others may now, for the first time, be developing a true appreciation for God's understanding love for them.

God wants to have a relationship with you and each member of your class. He sent His Son in order to make that relationship possible. What should you and your students do? There are many ways to respond to the truths that your class will examine in this session. Some may want to get to know God for the first time, to take advantage of the offer of a relationship with Christ. Others, who already have that relationship, may want to thank Him for what He did in reaching out to them, or to share that message with others. Some may wish to become more serious about their faith and/or about some Christian discipline that they need to strengthen.

Some of your students may not be ready for a relationship with God at the present time. They may realize that such a relationship will cost them something in terms of their friendships or activities. They may need to wrestle with God some more before they are ready to receive Him and enjoy His love.

In the Conclusion of this session your students will have an opportunity to respond to Christ. Some may wish to have further dialogue with you before making a decision, so make sure to contact those who have so indicated. Pray for those who have expressed needs and doubts. Be available to offer support to your learners in the spiritual struggles that they may face.

SESSION PLAN

BEFORE CLASS BEGINS: Photocopy the Gateway student worksheet and Fun Page take-home paper. See the CREATIVE ALTERNATIVE under the ATTENTION GRABBER for important instructions and materials required. The EXPLORATION also requires special preparation.

Attention Grabber

ATTENTION GRABBER (3-5 minutes)

Distribute paper and pencils. Have each student write a paragraph about a time that he or she came *close* to winning or achieving something good. After your class has finished ask, **What are some of the times that you have come close to winning or achieving something good?**

Allow a few students to share, then wrap up with something like this: **We have been talking about coming close to achieving something but yet missing it. The Bible tells us that this is the same kind of situation that everyone faces in having a relationship with God. You see, God is perfect. Imperfection cannot come into His presence, just as light cannot exist alongside darkness. Turn on a light and the darkness ceases. People are not perfect. If you doubt that, just look around. But God wants a relationship with us anyway. Today we are going to see what God has done in order to initiate that relationship with you that He wants to have.**

CREATIVE ALTERNATIVE (2-3 minutes)

Materials needed: Paper, envelopes, stamps, mailing list or addresses of class members (for a letter to be sent in advance of the class session).

Preparation: The week before this class session write a letter that says something like this: "Thank you for being a part of my class. As a reward for bringing this letter to class unopened, I want to invite you to have a Coke with me this week." (You can make the reward anything you like.) Make a copy of the letter for every student in your class. Fold the letter so that it cannot be read through the envelope if held up to a bright light. In bold letters on both the front and the back of the envelope write, "Bring this letter to class with you UNOPENED this Sunday morning." Send the letter so that it arrives early in the week before class.

When students arrive with their letters, ask, **How many of you can honestly say that you did not open your letter? How many of you tried to read your letter by holding it up to the light? How many of you tried to steam open your letter?**

After the class has responded, let them open the letters. Record the names of those who will be

NOTES

entitled to enjoy the reward. (Make sure you follow up on this.)

Tell your class, **You may be wondering what the point of this stunt was. I wanted to demonstrate to you how difficult it is for people to follow certain kinds of commandments. Most of you wanted to open the letter all the more just because it said not to, whereas if it were a piece of junk mail you might not have bothered to open it at all.**

If we had to please God with our own efforts in order to have a relationship with Him, we would have to follow His commands to the letter because God is perfect and can not allow imperfection into His presence. As you can tell from our experiment, it is very hard to obey even very simple commands. In fact, Jesus went so far as to say that if you even want to do something wrong it is the same, in the sense of rebellion, as if you had done it (although it may not have the same social consequences). It is this tendency to disobey, to do our own thing, that leads us to disobey God—to sin.

I think that this object lesson can help us see something about our own sinful nature. Today we are going to see what God did for us because of that sinful nature, how He went to the greatest lengths of love to establish a relationship with us.

Bible Exploration

EXPLORATION (25-35 minutes)

Before class begins, cut apart the 9 questions on the Teaching Resource page. Tape them in various places around the room—under chairs, on the ceiling, in the door jamb—any place that will be fun to locate.

Step 1 (1-2 minutes): Move students into groups of three to five and tell them, **Let's read Ephesians 2:1-10. In a few minutes you will be asked to answer nine questions about this passage.** Read the passage aloud (or have several volunteers read portions).

Step 2 (10-15 minutes): Say, **We are going to have a little contest that will be just for fun.** (If you think it will motivate your students more, offer a small reward.)

On your Gateway worksheet you will find the numbers one through nine. When I say go, I want you to search the classroom for a card with a question. Work as a group to answer it. (You may have to carry your Bible around with your finger in the passage we've just read.) **Then locate** another question hidden somewhere in the room and answer it. Remember to write full and complete answers on your worksheet, because we will be asking you to share them later. The object is to locate and correctly answer all the questions before we run out of time. Ready, set, go!

Keep track of the time and the progress of each group of students. If students are having a difficult time finding the answers, let them know they may not have time to complete all nine questions. If your class is streaking through the assignment, you may gain some extra time for Step 3. Be the timekeeper and periodically announce the time remaining.

When the time is up, have your students report their answers to the questions. If an answer is incorrect, ask the group to indicate where in the passage they got their response. Stimulate discussion on some answers by asking questions such as these: **How would most of the people you know respond to that statement? Which** part of the passage is the most difficult for people to understand? How would your school be different if all your friends understood and believed this passage? Comment as necessary, using material from INSIGHTS FOR THE LEADER.

Step 3 (12-15 minutes): Tell students, **Now, each group should come up with at least three slogans that could be developed from the verses that you've just read. These slogans should help people see how God has reached out to establish a relationship with us, and what we have to do or don't have to do to gain that relationship.**

(If your students have a hard time comprehending what you mean, give them an example from a secular company that has a slogan that summarizes what they want to do for the customer. Then give them an example from the text, like, "You don't deserve a break today—but God will give you one anyway." Remind them that the slogan doesn't have to be fancy or catchy but needs to communicate what God is doing to establish a relationship with us.)

Step 4 (3-4 minutes): Ask groups to share the slogans that they have created; write them on a sheet of newsprint or on the chalkboard as they are reported.

Conclusion and Decision

CONCLUSION (5-8 minutes)

Wrap up the lesson by saying something like this: **We have been looking at how God made possible a relationship with us through Christ. We have seen that there is nothing that we could do to help ourselves or to earn this relationship with Christ. I'd like you to take a look at "The Tie That Binds" section of the Gateway worksheet and prayerfully fill out that section. Then I'd like you to fold your Gateway worksheet in half and give it to me before you leave this morning.**

After your students have completed their worksheets, close in prayer. Collect the students' papers as they are going out the door. Distribute the Fun Page take-home paper.

This week, make sure to follow up on those who have indicated a desire for you to do so.

THE GATEWAY

Session 2

Nine Questions   You may need to use extra paper for your answers.

1.

2.

3.

4.

5.

6.

7.

8.

9.

The Tie That Binds
Please check the box that best describes your present relationship with Christ:

☐ I know Him . . . but we don't speak much.
☐ I've known Him for a long time but I'm starting to get doubts.
☐ I know the Lord and our relationship is great!
☐ I really don't understand much about all of this.
☐ I know all about Him, but I don't know Him.
☐ Other:

☐ I'd like to talk more about my relationship with God. (Write your name and phone number.)

Name _____   Phone _____

☐ I'm not ready to deal with this yet.

Cut the questions apart along the lines and hide them in your classroom as instructed in the EXPLORATION.

1. What is the description of the kind of spiritual life that we had when we followed the ways of the world?	2. Who did we follow before we were Christians? What is that another name for?	3. What was our inner nature before Christ changed us?
4. What did God do to show His love for us? Why was that a demonstration of His love?	5. What do you think the word grace means? (The Bible doesn't define it here but it gives lots of clues.)	6. From what you can figure out from this passage, who made the first move towards establishing a relationship between God and man? What was that move?
7. How does this passage say that we receive God's love, salvation and forgiveness?	8. What does this passage say about working our way towards salvation?	9. What were we created to do?

FUN Page!

Sleuth

The Nicodemus File   Case #John 3:1-16

REBORN? BORN TWICE? HOW CAN THESE THINGS BE?

ULP!

Jesus told Nicodemus that a person must be spiritually reborn in order to reach heaven.

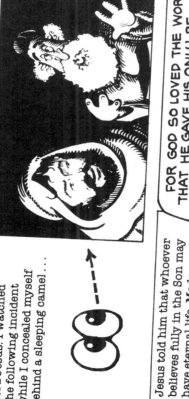

Jesus told him that whoever believes fully in the Son may have eternal life. Made sense to me.

FOR GOD SO LOVED THE WORLD, THAT HE GAVE HIS ONLY BE-GOTTEN SON, THAT WHOEVER BELIEVES IN HIM SHOULD NOT PERISH, BUT HAVE ETER-NAL LIFE!

Mug shot # 09309

09309

suspect: Nicodemus

Aliases: Nick the Pharisee; Lefty.

right thumb

It was a dark and scary night. I witnessed the religious Pharisee Nicodemus approach the Lord Jesus. I watched the following incident while I concealed myself behind a sleeping camel...

Sleuth's comment:

All the clues in this case lead to this conviction:
Anyone who truly believes and trusts in Jesus the Son will have ETERNAL LIFE with God in heaven!

HOT-THOT

"For it is by grace you have been saved, through faith—and this not from yourselves, it is the gift of God—not by works, so that no one can boast."
Ephesians 2:8,9

Well, the Nicodemus File on the other side of this paper tells us that Jesus Christ is the way to God and heaven. Most people already know that. But is there a way to heaven OTHER than Jesus?

Let's find out in this tongue-in-cheek look at the

Heavenly Maze

The object of the maze is to reach heaven (up in the clouds, of course). Even though there are several paths to take at the bottom of the maze, one and only one leads to heaven! Can you find it? (If you can't . . . well, you're not too sharp today!)

Being a good guy.

Maya the Shark Goddess.

Various philosophies of life.

JESUS!

Everybody goes.

Nobody goes.

WHAT KIND OF CRAZY MAZE IS THIS? ANYBODY CAN SEE THAT THE ONLY WAY TO HEAVEN IS THROUGH THE JESUS WAY!!!

EXACTLY!!!

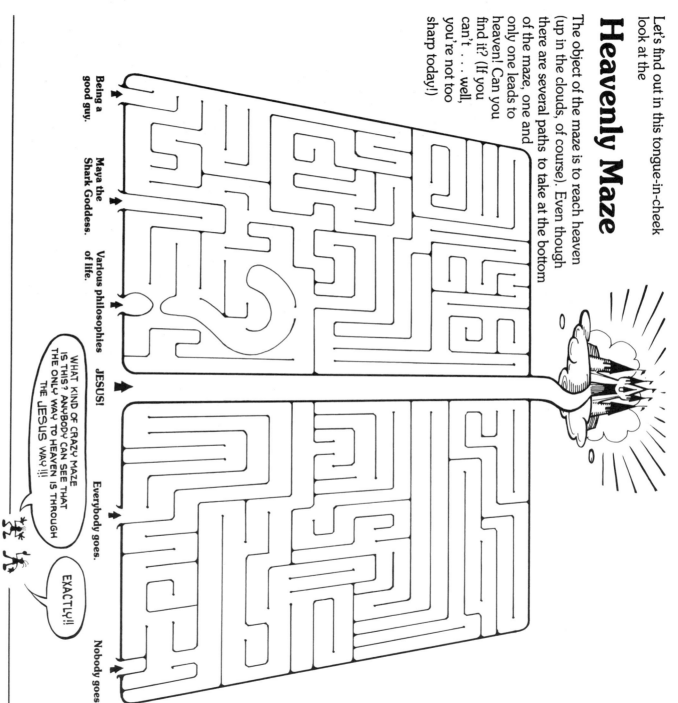

DAILY NUGGETS
Wisdom from God's Word for you to read each day.

Day 1 Read Ephesians 2:11-18. What has Jesus done, according to this passage? What does this mean for you personally?

Day 2 Romans 5:1. How is a person justified? What is one benefit faith brings?

Day 3 Ephesians 1:13,14. What happens as a result of one's believing the gospel message? What role of the Holy Spirit is described in these verses?

Day 4 1 John 1:9. When we confess our sins, what will the Lord do for us? If there is a particular sin in your life that you haven't yet told the Lord about, why not do so now in prayer?

Day 5 John 11:25. When we believe in Jesus, what does He give us?

Day 6 James 5:14-16. What is the Lord's response to those who have committed sin? How should we approach Jesus with our sins (vv. 15,16)?

THEME: Christ brings us to God.

Session 2

BIBLE STUDY OUTLINE

Read John 3:1-18 to your listeners. Make the following remarks as time permits.

Introductory remarks: Nicodemus was a man who looked like he had it all together. He was a religious leader, a man who should have been at peace with God and with himself. But he came to Jesus looking for answers. This is his story.

Verses 1-3: Perhaps Nicodemus came to Jesus at night because Jesus was such a busy man, or maybe because Nicodemus was nervous about being seen with the Lord. Jesus was a dynamic and controversial figure. Nicodemus knew He was a great teacher and a miracle worker. In response to Nicodemus's greeting, Jesus brought up an unexpected subject: being born again.

Jesus was able to go straight to the heart of Nicodemus's problem. Nick wasn't born again. He didn't even know what it meant.

Verses 4-8: Jesus explained by connecting the Holy Spirit to salvation. No one can enter heaven without a spiritual rebirth.

Each person is spiritually dead because of sin (see Rom. 6:23). That was Nick's problem, and that's our problem.

Verse 9: Nicodemus didn't understand what Jesus was talking about.

Verses 10-15: Nicodemus didn't understand that Jesus had come from heaven and that He must die so that all could have eternal life.

Verses 16-18: These verses describe the way to be born again. *(Now tell the True Story.)*

TRUE STORY: STRANGE BIRTH

(This story of a strange birth is presented to help illustrate the fact that there is only one way to be born into God's family. We do not condone all the procedures described.)

On September 28, 1987, Pat Anthony became the first woman in the world to give birth to her own grandchildren. When Pat's daughter was unable to have children through natural childbirth, Pat volunteered to act as a surrogate mother. So the daughter's eggs were mixed with the husband's sperm in a laboratory. The fertilized eggs were implanted in Pat's womb—and months later she gave birth to her daughter and son-in-law's triplets! Pat was 48 years old.

Modern science has enabled natural birth to be occasionally supplanted by so-called "test tube" births. Natural birth is also aided by medications designed to make the woman more fertile. Caesarean section operations allow the baby to be delivered through a cut in the mother's abdomen. All of these procedures allow babies to be born who never could have been born by natural birth.

But when it comes to being reborn—born again as Jesus said— there is only one way. Jesus is our Savior. There is no other way to reach eternal life. (Conclude by describing the need to be reborn and the best way to get started in the Christian life.)

DISCUSSION QUESTIONS

1. **Why wasn't Nicodemus good enough to reach heaven on his own?**

2. **In John 3:2, Nicodemus declares that he knows Jesus is from God. Why do you suppose this wasn't enough in Jesus' view to qualify for saving faith?**

3. **Who is the Holy Spirit and how are we related to Him?**

4. **Why did Jesus have to die?**

5. **What are some ways we can demonstrate our faith in God?**

THE COMPLETE
JUNIOR HIGH BIBLE STUDY
RESOURCE BOOK #5

Action games.

DOGS

You're probably familiar with the old coordinated clap game—the leader rhythmically waves his or her arms in the air and each time the hands cross, the members of the audience must clap their hands. The leader may suddenly stop waving; whoever claps is then out of the game.

This is a variation of that game. Whenever a player claps out of turn, he or she is not only eliminated from the game but also must get on all fours and bark like a dog for a few seconds. The next time someone is eliminated, he or she must bark—but so must all the players who were dogs before. Soon almost everyone will be barking. It's a riot.

TIGER BY THE TAIL

Players form a conga line—a single file line with each player placing his or her hands on the waist of the player ahead. The lead player has hands free; the object is for the lead player to catch the last player in the line. The last player tries to avoid capture. Anyone who breaks the line is eliminated. When the lead player catches the last player, the person behind the lead player becomes the new leader. This way, everyone gets a chance to be the head and the tail of the tiger.

HITCH THE CABOOSE

This game requires at least eight players and a large amount of space. Players form conga lines of three or more people each. You need at least two lines, but the more the merrier. Two players remain free; they are not in any group (if you have a large number of lines, add a few more loose players).

At the signal, the conga lines run all over the area. The loose players try to attach themselves to the end of the lines. If a loose player captures a line, the first player in the line becomes a loose caboose.

Undivided Loyalty

WHAT THE SESSION IS ABOUT

There is a significant difference between believing the facts in the Bible, and personally risking oneself in a relationship with Christ.

SCRIPTURE STUDIED

Joshua 24:14,15; 1 Kings 18:17-21; 2 Kings 17:32-41; Matthew 6:24; James 1:26,27; 2:14-18

KEY PASSAGE

"How long will you waver between two opinions? If the Lord is God, follow him; but if Baal is God, follow him." 1 Kings 18:21

AIMS OF THE SESSION

During this session your learners will:
1. Examine biblical incidents of faltering faith;
2. List areas in which junior highers tend to have divided loyalties;
3. Test what they say they believe about Christ against their actions.

INSIGHTS FOR THE LEADER

There are many reasons why your junior highers are in Sunday School. Some are there because their parents make them come. Others come because they'll see their friends there. Some attend in spite of their parents' apathy—even against their parents' wishes—because they are attracted to Christ. Some students may be your friends who are there only because a special person—you—asked them to come to Sunday School.

Most of your learners will say they come because they believe in Jesus Christ and want to learn about the Bible. That is the usual and accepted reason for being in Sunday School. None, or almost none, of your students would say, "I don't believe in God or Jesus."

Junior highers may assume that they believe in Christ because they have no argument with the facts in the Bible. But are they relying on the Lord for salvation and for everyday strength? Are they clinging to Christ rather than to the appeal of things around them? Do they trust Jesus—or do they trust friends' opinions as their guide for life? Believing in the Scriptures means relying on, clinging to, trusting rather than simply "saying it's true."

Trying to believe in Christ without going out on a limb with Him will result in living in two worlds at once. Your students will study several people in the Bible who attempted to acknowledge God's way while following another way at the same time. It didn't work.

God told them to make up their minds! He preferred that they definitely go away from Him rather than waver between Him and idolatry.

A person who clearly turns away from the Lord has made up his mind—and can change his mind. If he has gone away, he can turn and come back. But a person who tries to do both at once will give you a blank stare if you say, "Wouldn't you like to follow Christ?" He thinks he already is following Christ.

That's why you don't need to panic, or think all is lost, if you have junior high learners who are openly belligerent toward the gospel. At least they know where they are, and you know where they are. They may be more reachable than the learners who say placidly, "Sure I believe," but who live just like their unsaved friends.

But suppose you have a class full of those semi-sincere kids! Today's session will lead them through an exercise that tests what they say they believe against what their actions demonstrate. That is the real test of belief (see Jas. 2:17,18).

In this session your students will examine several biblical passages dealing with the importance of making a conscious choice either for or against God. The following background material will help you guide your learners as they explore God's Word.

NOTES

King Ahab

The first passage is 1 Kings 18:17-21. King Ahab ruled Israel between 871 and 851 B.C. He "did more evil in the eyes of the Lord than any of those before him . . . . He set up an altar for Baal in the temple of Baal that he built in Samaria" (1 Kings 16:30,32). In the midst of all this royally-sanctioned idolatry God called the prophet Elijah and sent him to set Israel straight. Ahab called him "you troubler of Israel" (1 Kings 18:17), but idolatry was Israel's real trouble.

Elijah challenged the prophets of Baal (a fertility god) to a duel. The excitement of this challenge drew a large crowd, eager to see something spectacular. Elijah took advantage of the presence of these people to confront them with their lack of commitment to one side or another. He demanded, "How long will you waver between two opinions?" (1 Kings 18:21)."Waver" in the *NIV*, or "hesitate" in the *NASB*, is "halt" in the *KJV*. But "halt" did not mean "stop" as it means today. "Halt" meant "lame," or "to limp." Elijah's question has been translated, "How long do you mean to hobble first on one leg then on the other?" (*JB*), "How much longer will it take you to make up your minds?" (*TEV*). Quoting these different translations will help clear up the natural confusion your learners may have over the term "halt" if they are reading the *KJV*—besides restating the basic question in several colorful ways.

God and Idols

In 2 Kings 17:32-41, learners will read of another time when the Israelites tried to worship God along with idols. Israel was conquered by King Shalmaneser of Assyria in 722 B.C., about 150 years after Elijah's challenge. To break up the Israelites' unity, Shalmaneser exported many of the Jews and imported people from other conquered nations to populate Israel (see 2 Kings 17:6,18,24). When the immigrants began to suffer misfortune, the king's advisors told him it was because they "do not know what the god of that country requires" (17:26). So the king said, "Have one of the priests you took captive from Samaria go back to live there and teach the people what the god of the land requires" (17:27). A Jewish priest was sent back from exile to teach the newcomers about God. But the result was that "they worshiped the Lord, but they also served their own gods in accordance with the customs of the nations from which they had been brought.Even while these people were worshiping the Lord, they were serving their idols" (17:33,41).

Joshua 24:14,15

Moses' successor, Joshua, led the Israelites to victory over the inhabitants of Canaan, the land God had promised to them. When he was about to die, Joshua reminded the people of God's faithfulness and the necessity of being faithful to Him in return. He was concerned that after his death Israel would abandon God to follow the idols of the Canaanites.

"Be very strong; be careful to obey all that is written in the Book of the Law of Moses, without turning aside to the right or to the left. Do not associate with these nations that remain among you; do not invoke the names of their gods or swear by them. You must not serve them or bow down to them. But you are to hold fast to the Lord your God, as you have until now" (Josh. 23:6-8).

The passage which the students will read in this session is Joshua 24:14,15: "Now fear the Lord and serve him with all faithfulness. Throw away the gods your forefathers worshiped beyond the River and in Egypt, and serve the Lord. But if serving the Lord seems undesirable to you, then choose for yourselves this day whom you will serve, whether the gods your forefathers served beyond the River, or the gods of the Amorites, in whose land you are living. But as for me and my household, we will serve the Lord."

Joshua put a choice to the people: make up your mind whether to serve God or not, and if you won't serve God, decide whom you will serve! ("The River" is the Jordan River which they had crossed to enter Canaan; "beyond the River" therefore means on the other side of the Jordan, where they had come from, the wilderness.)

Notice that Joshua knew the stand he would take no matter what the rest of the people did: "But as for me and my household, we will serve the Lord" (v. 15).

There are many other biblical passages having to

do with deciding for or against the Lord—and not trying to serve both. Jesus made it very clear that serving God was incompatible, not just with worshiping idols, but with the love of earthly riches. James emphasized that claims to serve God are invalidated by lives marked with immoral speech or lack of charitable actions. Other passages reinforce this truth: Revelation 3:14-16 ("I would that you were cold or hot," *NASB*); Deuteronomy 30:15-19 ("See, I set before you today life and prosperity, death and destruction").

The biblical principle for junior high students— and for adults—is that God wants us to make up our minds whether to serve Him or not. Perhaps one of your junior highers has made up his mind against God for now. Don't write him off! He is probably more open to talking about Christ than your students who are still "limping." He has made a conscious decision; he can make another conscious decision and accept Christ. Those who haven't really decided what they want to believe are susceptible to the latest fad in thinking. This session will help them face their inconsistencies, and consider what they need to do in response.

SESSION PLAN

BEFORE CLASS BEGINS: Photocopy the Gateway student worksheet and the Fun Page take-home paper. Photocopy the Teaching Resource page (one for each student) and cut the copies along the center line. The OPTIONAL *STEP 3* of the EXPLORATION suggests you bring samples of editorial cartoons to class.

Attention Grabber

ATTENTION GRABBER (5-6 minutes)

Direct your students' attention to the "Jaws Revisited" section of the Gateway worksheet. Spend some time discussing what your students would do in a similar situation and why. Make a transition by saying something like this: **We've seen by many of your responses that most of you would believe with such intensity that it would produce action—in this case heading for dry ground. Today we are going to look at this idea from a spiritual perspective. We are going to see some examples of people whose actions did not always match up with their declared beliefs.**

Bible Exploration

EXPLORATION (25-50 minutes)

Step 1 (2-3 minutes): Distribute the "Belief Quiz" portion of the Teaching Resource page. Tell students, **You will find some statements you can mark either "I believe it" or "I don't believe it." You either believe each one or you don't. By the way, I'm not going to check your answers. Mark honestly what you believe and do not believe.**

Step 2 (7-10 minutes): Lead a discussion based on the "Don't Choose a Loser" section of the Gateway. Tell students to write down the answers as the discussion progresses. Variation: Assemble your class into small groups to work the assignment.

OPTIONAL STEP 3 (10-15 minutes): Tell your students, **I'd like you to draw an editorial-type cartoon that demonstrates the disloyalty, indecision, unsteadiness or division these people experienced.** (It would be good to show some examples clipped from a newspaper.) Have the groups share their completed cartoons. Make sure to write any good insights on your chalkboard.

Step 4 (3-5 minutes): Say, **There are many areas in which people can have divided loyalties.** Give an example from your own life. **Tell me some of the ways people your age have divided loyalties.** List their responses on the chalkboard. **Now you will take a short quiz to help you determine whether or not you have any divided loyalties.**

Step 5 (7-10 minutes): Now distribute the "I Do" portion of the Teaching Resource page. Tell students, **Mark your true, honest, confidential answers to all those statements.**

When learners have completed "I Do," read aloud this passage from Matthew 6:24: **"No one can serve two masters. Either he will hate the one and love the other, or he will be devoted to the one and despise the other."** Also read James 2:17,18: **"Faith by itself, if it is not accompanied by action, is dead . . .I will show you my faith by what I do."**

Say something like this: **James says that what we do shows what we really believe. Real faith in Jesus will always show in our lives. But lack of faith in Jesus is also bound to show in our lives. And Jesus Himself said it has to be one or the other. That sounds like a hard thing to decide, doesn't it? To tell the truth, our actions—how we live—already show what we put our faith and trust in.**

Have the learners compare the two portions of the Teaching Resource page.

Explain, **Read each of the questions and answers. Are there any places where you're divided? In other words, is what you said you believed in the quiz really confirmed by what you do according to the "I Do" section? Here's an example. Say you marked "Good grades are very important—I don't believe it." That should be confirmed by how much you study. Do you study "never"? Then you're right—you don't believe good grades are important. If you said you believe grades are important, but you study "never," can we really believe you think grades are that important? Or for instance, did you mark "God hears and answers my prayers—I believe it"? Okay, then what do your actions in prayer show? Are you "limping" between two opinions? If you almost never pray, but you say you believe God hears and answers—**

do you really believe He'll hear and answer you? Then why don't you pray more? That would be an example of wavering between two things, like Elijah said.

Encourage learners to focus on items 2,4,5,7 and 8, to evaluate their relationship with God.

Let the learners read through all they have written, and don't be afraid of silence, even if it goes on for a while. Remind them that this is all confidential between them and the Lord.

Step 6 (5-10 minutes): Say, **In closing we'll read a little more of James. He was a very** practical man. He knew the difference between talk and action.

Read James 1:26,27 and 2:14-18, or have a student read the portion.

Ask questions such as these: **What does James have to say about saying one thing and doing another? What does this say about going back and forth between two opinions? It doesn't use those exact words, but can you find the same idea?**

How does this apply to your answers to the "I DO" quiz?

Conclusion and Decision

CONCLUSION (3-5 minutes)

Tell students, **Think back over any beliefs and actions about which you are inconsistent. Which way do you really want to go? Joshua said, "Choose for yourselves this day whom you will serve." You can decide today which way to go and stop splitting yourself between two opinions. And you can make some plans to follow Christ in that area of your life.**

Let students pray silently and write a brief note describing their prayer. Have them fold and keep their notes.

Before closing in prayer, tell students you will stick around after class to talk with any of them who are interested in choosing to serve the Lord, or any who want to know more about what a commitment to Christ means.

Distribute the Fun Page as students leave.

THE GATEWAY

— A True Story — JAWS REVISITED —

The water was warm and crystal clear as Barry and I paddled our surfboards into the breakers. We stroked over the sandy bottom, watching the minnows swimming under us. Finally reaching a point beyond the impact zone of the curling waves, we sat and waited for the larger swells to come in.

Suddenly Barry cried, "Look at that!" Through the transparent emerald water a six-foot-plus shark was swimming slowly up the beach. Sitting less than seven feet away, we froze in an odd combination of fear, awe, surprise and shock at the sight of the grey creature moving past us. We stared at him until we could no longer see him cutting his slow path through the midst of the surfers gathered on that summer morning. But we could tell where he was by the peculiar behavior that overtook those who spotted him.

Barry and I debated what to do. Good sense dictated that we head for the sand, but beautiful waves can do funny things to your sensibilities. If you were in a similar situation what would you do? Why?

Don't Choose a Loser

1 1 Kings 18:17-21

Ahab did more evil in the sight of God than any king before him. Rather than worship the true God he set up temples to the god Baal. (To learn more about this loser, see the Scripture indicated below.) He also made an image to the goddess Asherah. This was in direct disobedience to the law of God. Baal is the most frequently mentioned idol in the Bible. Baal was actually a word that meant "master" or "Lord." Whatever god happened to be the object of worship was usually referred to as Baal in the Bible, because the "first name" or title of the god of the sun, moon, stars, rain, etc., usually started with the word "Baal."

What was it that Elijah said when he went before the people?

What was the people's initial response?

What was the reason that Elijah gave for the trouble that Israel had found herself in?

2 2 Kings 17:32-41

The king of Assyria brought people from various countries to resettle Samaria. The people of God were surrounded by those who had different values and worshiped false gods.

The king decided to have the people worship their own gods. This gave the Israelites a chance to tell everyone about the true God, which they did. But many people, including some of God's people, worshiped the false gods as well. It was into this mess that the Word of God came down loud and clear.

The people here worshiped both the true God of Israel and _____

What was the covenant or agreement that God made with the children of Israel?

3 Joshua 24:14,15

Many of God's people began to adopt the ways of idol worshipers. Joshua gathered all the people and reminded them of what God had done for them. He sternly warned them to get rid of the idols they were worshiping. You'll be examining a part of that speech below.

Some of these gods required small children to be burned alive as sacrifices. Some of the gods required only a token gift once in a while to keep them happy. But it is pretty clear why these "gods" can be considered false. We still have people who worship false gods today but we don't call them Baal worshipers. They worship false gods like money, sex, pleasure or ego.

What did Joshua suggest that the people do with all the gods that they had been worshiping?

What decision did Joshua demand from his people?

What decision did Joshua's family make?

Belief Quiz ■ I Do

Answer the questions below honestly.

I study: ☐ constantly ☐ seldom

I pray: ☐ when I'm in trouble ☐ seldom ☐ often

I don't mind if I wear out-of-date clothes: ☐ true ☐ false

I watch TV for about _____ hours per day.

What I love most of all is: _____

The last time I said, "Thanks" to my folks was: _____

I read God's Word: ☐ often ☐ seldom

I feel I should change _____ before God will let me go to heaven.

I believe it!   I don't believe it!

1. Good grades are very important to get.
_____ _____

2. God hears and answers my prayers.
_____ _____

3. Being accepted at school is vital.
_____ _____

4. My time belongs to God.
_____ _____

5. Christ is first in my life.
_____ _____

6. It is important to show gratitude.
_____ _____

7. The Bible is a dependable guide for my life.
_____ _____

8. I believe Jesus Christ died for all my sins.
_____ _____

Session 3

Old Tired Yokes File

Once upon a time there was a chicken. It must have been a girl chicken, since to my knowledge there is no such thing as a guy chicken.

Her name was Gertrude. Gertrude the chicken.

One day Gertrude the chicken decided she wanted to cross the road. Why, you may ask, did the chicken cross...

OH, NO YOU DON'T! I AIN'T FALLING FOR **THAT** OLD JOKE!

Well, to make a long chicken story short...

HEY, DID YOU HEAR ABOUT THE TRUCK THAT RAN OVER THE **HENWAY**?

WHAT'S A HENWAY?

OH, ABOUT **EIGHT POUNDS!!**

THAT'S PROBABLY THE **WORST** JOKE I'VE EVER HEARD!

POP! PUTT! ACME FARMS

Anyway, Gertrude the chicken had made up her little chicken mind. She took a deep breath, looked both ways, and ran across the road as fast as her little drumsticks could carry her.

HEY, THIS IS EASY! WHY SHOULD I HURRY? I'M NOT EVEN SURE I WANT TO CROSS THE ROAD! I'LL JUST STAY HERE ON THE ROAD WHERE I CAN ENJOY THE VIEW OF **BOTH** SIDES!!

The old men in the old truck put an end to Gertrude the chicken's indecision. Sooner or later each and every person must decide what to do with Jesus; whether to stay on the side of the road and ignore Him, or to cross the road and love and follow Him!

Unfortunately, many chickens—er, people I mean—try to sit in the middle of the road enjoying both worlds!

It's got to be one or the other. Either follow Jesus wholeheartedly, or ignore Him totally. Otherwise you'll be like Gertrude. Enjoying nothing.

Choose, if you haven't already, which side of the road you want to be on! Don't be a dumb chuck!

Drawing a Blank

Just for fun (and maybe to learn something about yourself too) fill in the blanks below to form a sentence that states what you really think about commitment to the Lord Jesus.

Instructions: Each numbered blank has a similarly numbered card which contains six word phrases. Choose one phrase from each card to go in each appropriate blank.

I, 1 _____ _____ that it's important to commit my _2 _____ _____ to Jesus even

though _3 _____ and _4 _____ , because _5 _____ _____

and _6 _____ !

1	2	3
strongly believe read in the Sleuth once wrote on the wall keep forgetting have been told every week read in a fortune cookie	life dog sister teacher Sunday mornings vast wealth	I'm young I'm dumb I would never fill in this blank I don't know what I'm talking about I thought "commit" was a meteor in space, like Halley's Commit I would rather go to the beach

4	5	6

my friends may think I'm wrong
this is a stupid game
this must be a nightmare
I can't go on with this nonsense
I hope nobody sees me playing
  this game
I'm going crazy
	I love Him
	I'm just so nice a person
	otherwise my mom will kill me
	the Martians are coming to get me
	the world ends tomorrow
	I'm bored
		He loves me
		I want to go to heaven
		I learned a lot from Gertrude the
		  chicken
		I'm smart, that's why
		I'll turn into a french fry if I don't
		I'm never going to read THE FUN
		  PAGE again

Now that you've had some fun, fill in the blanks with the phrases (or your own original words) that describe what you seriously believe about Jesus. You may want to keep the finished sentence handy as a reminder to you about your beliefs.

DAILY NUGGETS

Day 1 Read Matthew 13:10-15. Explain in your own words what Jesus meant by this apparent contradiction or paradox. Why do you think people can hear about Christ or His teaching and not apply to their lives what they hear?

Day 2 Matthew 13:15-17. From what these verses say, do you think that these people's rejection of God's teaching comes from ignorance or from intentionally closing their minds?

Day 3 Matthew 9:9. Who contacted Matthew? What was Matthew's job? What did he leave to follow Christ?

Day 4 Matthew 9:10-12. To what professional does Jesus compare Himself? See if you can write out a "prescription for sin."

Day 5 Luke 9:57-60. What was Jesus trying to say to these people? Ask somebody what it means to "let the dead bury their own dead."

Day 6 Luke 9:61,62. What do you think the cost is to follow Christ? Consider and rewrite these verses.

THE FUN

"How long will you waver between two opinions? If the Lord is God, follow him; but if Baal is God, follow him."
1 Kings 18:21

THEME: Undivided loyalty to God.

Session 3

BIBLE STUDY OUTLINE

Read the following passages about Judas Iscariot to your students.

Matthew 26:14-16: Judas Iscariot is the most famous traitor the world has ever known. If someone betrays us, we call that person a Judas. How is it that Judas Iscariot—one of the 12 men who were Christ's closest friends here on earth—became such a horrible traitor? The same way that it is possible for anyone to fall away from God: a lack of commitment to Him. Divided loyalties. Judas betrayed Jesus because he couldn't resist the attraction of money. He wanted the silver coins. Today, people just like you and me fall away from God for money, for romance, for power—for any and every reason. The big question is: Is it worth it? Let's take a look at what happened to Judas.

Matthew 27:3-5: Judas hanged himself out of remorse. He lost the joy he could have known as a friend of Christ, he lost the money and he lost his life. He lost everything that he had—all because he didn't remain loyal to Jesus. This is an important lesson for all believers to learn and remember. God demands our loyalty. We mustn't make the mistake of trying to live for Him only part time. He expects us to walk with Him full time. That's the secret to a successful Christian life.

Acts 1:23-25: The believers were gathered to elect a new apostle to take the place of the dead Judas. Notice that verse 25 states that Judas left to "go where he belongs." Where is that? It ain't heaven! It is possible for a person to know all about Jesus like Judas apparently did, yet to never know him as Lord and Savior. Each Christian must examine his or her own heart to see if true loyalty to God is there. If not, it's time to make it right. *(Now do the Object Lesson.)*

OBJECT LESSON:

Objects needed: a magnet, a metal object to stick the magnet to, a match or lighter.

Show your audience the magnet. Describe how magnets stick to any ferrous metal and demonstrate by sticking the magnet to the metal object. Explain that Christians should stick close to God like a magnet to metal—but sometimes Christians are more attracted to other things. Judas was attracted to money.

Now light the match or lighter. Tell your listeners that a magnet can be ruined by high temperature. The heat destroys the magnetic attraction. (The match or lighter isn't hot enough to do so, however.) Say something like, **Perhaps this is why God sometimes allows us to be burned when we give in to the temptations of this world. Enough heat may make us lose our attraction to the things of this world. Instead, we'll cling to Him.**

Give students an opportunity to silently commit themselves to the Lord in prayer.

DISCUSSION QUESTIONS

1. **What does it mean to be betrayed?**

2. **Why do you think Judas betrayed Jesus? Why do you suppose it's hard for some people to remain loyal to God in their Christian walk? Is this a common problem?**

3. **What are some things a Christian can do to grow strongly loyal to Jesus?**

4. **What are some things we as a group can do to help each other out?**

THE COMPLETE
JUNIOR HIGH BIBLE STUDY
RESOURCE BOOK #5

Some time-wasters for long bus trips.

GOING DOTTY

A game for two players. Draw a bunch of dots in rows on a sheet of paper. To take a turn, a player draws a line connecting a dot with its neighbor. The line may be drawn in any direction except diagonally and it may be drawn anywhere on the paper. When the line is drawn, it is the next player's turn.

The object is to connect the dots to form small squares. The player who draws a line to complete a square places his or her initial in the square and then draws an additional line anywhere. The player who forms the most squares wins.

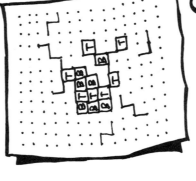

CRAZY QUILT

A game for two to four players. Draw a bunch of dots on a sheet of paper, just as in the game above. As before, players are to connect a dot to its neighbor with a short line. However, the object this time is not to form boxes, but to form one long line that never connects to itself. No diagonal lines, no skipped spaces and no branches off the main line. The winner is the one who draws the last line without connecting the long line to itself.

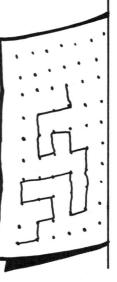

TWENTY BIBLE QUESTIONS

Don't forget the good old game of Twenty Questions. One player thinks of a subject and then tells the other player if it's animal, vegetable or mineral. The animal category includes any kind of animal, person or groups thereof. The mineral category is anything that is not plant or animal. To play Twenty Bible Questions, players must choose subjects from the Bible. If the subject was Christ's cross, the category would be plant (wood) and the guessing player would have twenty questions (yes or no answers only) in which to identify the subject.

WHAT THE SESSION IS ABOUT

Because Christ offers His friendship to us, we can respond in ways that build up our relationship with Him.

SCRIPTURE STUDIED

Matthew 12:1-4; 14:22-33; 26:48-50; Mark 4:34; 6:30-32; 9:30,31; 14:3-9,32-38; Luke 8:51-55; 10:38-42; 24:36-43; John 1:35-39; 11:1-6,17-26; 13:1-5; 15:12-17; 18:4-9; 20:11-16; 21:4-13

KEY PASSAGE

"You are my friends if you do what I command. I no longer call you servants, because a servant does not know his master's business. Instead, I have called you friends, for everything that I learned from my Father I have made known to you." John 15:14,15

AIMS OF THE SESSION

1. Examine biblical accounts of ways Christ kept friendships close;

2. List specific actions that help or hinder a person's friendship with Christ;

3. Plan to respond in one way that will build up their friendship with Christ.

INSIGHTS FOR THE LEADER

The problem with any session on keeping close to God is that your junior highers probably already know all the answers: they are aware that they should pray, read the Bible, obey what the Lord tells them to do, attend worship, share Christ with other people.

Then why do so many junior high students fall flat in fulfilling those requirements for keeping close to God? For the same reason that many adults do—they don't have enough incentive to put out the amount of effort required. After all (they reason), God is always with me and I'm already forgiven in Christ. Besides (they also think), when I do make the effort to do the right things, I may not feel any closer to God, so what difference does it make to follow all those rules?

Close Friends

This session approaches keeping close from an angle of friendship. Friendship is extremely important to your students. Being accepted by friends is crucial, and the loss of a friend is traumatic. Junior highers have no trouble seeing the importance of a good friendship—and little trouble figuring out what must be done to keep a friendship strong.

Christ offers His friendship to your junior highers. During this session, they will examine some ways in which He acted as a friend to people of His day and will draw from these actions some principles of friendship. Then they will consider how their own actions are helping or hindering their relationship with Him.

The Scriptures in the "Scripture Studied" for this session are quite brief. The learning activity does not require students to read every Scripture.

The paragraphs below deal with all the Scriptures for the lesson, giving a brief statement of the main points of each passage. Study this material in order to be prepared to share with your students the friend who is Jesus.

Matthew 12:1-4—Jesus defended His friends, the disciples, against accusations.

Matthew 14:22-33—Jesus came to His friends when they were in trouble; He reassured them; He rescued Peter when he failed; He quieted the storm that endangered them.

Matthew 26:48-50—He was still able to call Judas "friend" even as Judas handed Him over to guards; He never gave up on His friend.

Mark 4:34—He took them into His confidence.

Mark 6:30-32—Jesus took His friends away to rest when they were tired; He was sensitive to the pressures on them.

Mark 9:30,31—He avoided other involvements to take special time with them.

Mark 14:3-9—He defended a friend against ridicule and explained why she acted as she did.

Mark 14:32-38—Jesus singled out special friends to be with Him when He suffered; He was merciful when they failed Him.

Luke 8:51-55—He singled out special friends to be with Him at a "private" miracle; He trusted them.

Luke 10:38-42—He encouraged His friends to be quiet and to listen to and learn from Him.

Luke 24:36-43—He made Himself available for them to test the reality of His resurrection; He did not remain distant and aloof.

John 1:35-39—He extended hospitality; invited them to spend time with Him where He lived.

John 11:1-6,17-26—Jesus delayed His answer so their faith could grow; He made a promise He could keep.

John 13:1-5—Jesus served His friends with humility; He lowered Himself to a slave's job.

John 15:12-17—He let them know what He expected; He offered intimate knowledge of Himself; He encouraged them to love each other.

John 18:4-9—He tried to protect his friends from arrest even while He was being arrested.

John 20:11-16—Jesus came to Mary personally, called her by name, reassured her that He was alive.

John 21:4-13—He showed concern for their discouragement, made breakfast, spent time with them to show He was alive.

The Scriptures examined in this session, though not exhaustive, give a good picture of the kind of friend Jesus Christ was and is. As students grow in their understanding of the friendship He offers, many will respond by choosing to build up their relationship with Him.

SESSION PLAN

BEFORE CLASS BEGINS: Photocopy the Gateway and Fun Page.

Attention Grabber

ATTENTION GRABBER (1-2 minutes)

Write the word "FRIEND" in large capital letters on the chalkboard. Say, **The word *friend* has six letters in it. On a blank piece of paper, I want you to write a six-word sentence in which each word starts with a letter from our word *friend*. Your sentence can be funny, serious, or anywhere in between. Work together in pairs.**

Examples: From Ruin Indeed, Even Now Despair; Funny Rubber Icicles Encourage Nose Drops.

After a couple of minutes, ask volunteers to share their answers.

Make a transition to the Bible Exploration part of the session by saying something like this: **Jesus Christ offered His friendship to many people, but they had to respond to Him and make up their minds to be His friends. Let's look at how Jesus extended friendship to people and how He dealt with His friends.**

Bible Exploration

NOTES

EXPLORATION (25-35 minutes)

Step 1 (10-15 minutes): Have students form groups of four to five. Direct attention to the "Friends of Jesus" section of the Gateway. Tell students, **Working together in your groups, look up the Scripture references in the Gateway and match them to the correct description of Christ's actions in the other column. Do as many as you can until I tell you to stop.**

Have some groups start at the top of the list and some at the bottom.

(If you have a small class, let students work as individuals to match as many Scriptures as they can in the time allowed.)

Step 2 (10-12 minutes): Reassemble the class. Go over the matching exercise, providing the correct match-ups and commenting on several ways in which Jesus demonstrated His friendship. Use material from the INSIGHTS FOR THE LEADER. Ask students, **Why does this type of action build friendship?**

Step 3 (5-6 minutes): Ask something like this: **Can you think of ways people respond to Christ that hurt their friendship with Him? Ways that let it cool off? What are some better ways to respond to Him?**

List responses on the chalkboard under "Building Friendship" and "Dismantling Friendship" headings. Ask questions such as, **Why is it easy to fall into patterns that dismantle rather than build friendship? What can we do when the good things that build friendship seem dry or unproductive?** Let students wrestle with these questions and find answers that are meaningful to them.

Make a transition to the Conclusion by saying something like, **Our actions and attitudes tend to do one of two things—hurt our relationship with Jesus or help it. How we think and act is not an accident. We can make definite plans to do things that will help our friendship with the Lord grow.**

Conclusion and Decision

CONCLUSION (3 minutes)

Tell students, **Find the "Warm-Up Plans" on the Gateway. Answer this for yourself: What have I been doing, thinking or saying that tends to hurt my relationship with Christ? Take time to think it over and write in your answer where it says, "I've been cooling off my friendship with Christ by:" Now what will you do to help further your relationship with the Lord? Write what you plan to do where it** says, **"I plan to warm up my friendship with Christ by:" and, if you can make it even more detailed and specific, write a very particular action where it says, "I'm going to take this action."**

Close in prayer asking God to give your learners the courage to carry out their plans. Thank Him for His faithful friendship.

Distribute the Fun Page.

■ Friends of Jesus ■

Match the Scripture with the event that demonstrated Christ's friendship.

Matthew 12:1-4
Matthew 14:22-33
Matthew 26:48-50
Mark 4:34
Mark 6:30-32
Mark 9:30,31
Mark 14:3-9
Mark 14:32-38
Luke 8:51-55
Luke 10:38-42
Luke 24:36-43
John 1:35-39
John 11:1-6,17-26
John 13:1-5
John 15:12-17
John 18:4-9
John 20:11-16
John 21:4-13

> "You are my friends if you do what I command. I no longer call you servants, because a servant does not know his master's business. Instead, I have called you friends, for everything that I learned from my Father I have made known to you."
> John 15:14,15

Warm-Up Plans

I've been cooling off my friendship with Christ by:

I plan to warm up my friendship with Christ by:

And that means I'm going to take this action:

Defended a friend against ridicule and explained why she acted as she did.

Singled out special friends to be with Him when He suffered; was merciful when they failed Him.

Singled out special friends to be with Him at a "private" miracle; trusted them.

Tried to protect them from arrest even while He was being arrested.

Let them know what He expected; offered intimate knowledge of Himself; encouraged them to love each other.

Served them with humility; lowered Himself to a slave's job.

Encouraged His friends to be quiet and listen to and learn from Him.

Made Himself available for them to test whether He had risen from the dead; did not remain distant and aloof.

Extended hospitality and invited them to spend time with Him where He lived.

Delayed His answer so their faith could grow; made a promise He could keep.

Defended His friends, the disciples, against accusations.

Took them into His confidence.

Took them away to rest when they were tired; sensitive to the pressures on them.

Avoided other involvements to take special time with them.

Came to His friends when they were in trouble; reassured them; rescued Peter when he failed; quieted the storm that endangered them.

Came to Mary personally, called her by name, reassured her that He was alive.

Showed concern for their discouragement, made breakfast, spent time with them to show He was alive.

Was still able to call Judas "friend" even as Judas handed Him over to guards; never gave up on His friend.

The Mother and Brothers File:

Case # Matthew 12:46-50

Jesus was preaching to the multitudes. It was easy for me to observe the situation while I concealed myself in the crowds. Here's what I saw:

While Jesus was speaking, His mother and brothers came to Him.

I thought it was a strange question. Didn't He know?

WHO IS MY MOTHER AND WHO ARE MY BROTHERS?

Someone told Jesus His family was there.

YOUR MOTHER AND BROTHERS ARE HERE.

FOR WHOEVER SHALL DO THE WILL OF MY FATHER WHO IS IN HEAVEN, HE IS MY BROTHER AND SISTER AND MOTHER.

Jesus pointed His hand at the entire crowd and said that THEY were His mother and brothers!

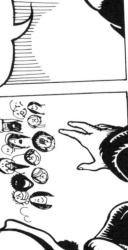

Sleuth's comment:

After weighing the evidence, I conclude that any person who is a believer in Jesus Christ is more than just an acquaintance of His— that person is actually a MEMBER of God's FAMILY!

FAMILY RELATIONS

We know that each and every Christian is a member of God's family. God is our Father, and Christ calls us His closest relations—"For whoever does the will of my Father in heaven is my brother and sister and mother" (Matthew 12:50).

But can you figure out what relation to you these people are?

1. Father's brother's uncle's sister.
2. Niece's father's only brother.
3. Aunt's mother's father's wife.
4. Aunt's mother's only grandchild.
5. Sister's mother's father.
6. Grandmother's sister's daughter's son.
7. Husband's sister's daughter's son.

That ought to be enough to drive you cross-eyed! The answers are below.

Answers: 1. Grandaunt or grandmother. 2. Self, brother, or no relation. 3. Great-grandmother. 4. Self. 5. Grandfather. 6. Cousin. 7. Grandnephew.

DAILY NUGGETS

Day 1 Read John 10:27-29. What does Jesus give to His followers (sheep)?

Day 2 Psalm 37:3-6. According to these verses what can we do to be close to the Lord? When we do these things, what will God do?

Day 3 John 15:4,5. What happens when we abide (remain) in Christ?

Day 4 Colossians 3:16,17. How are we to let Christ's Word dwell within us? What does v. 17 tell us about the attitude we should have in all our actions?

Day 5 1 Peter 2:2,3. What is the "milk" mentioned in this verse? How do you get the "milk"?

Day 6 2 Timothy 3:14-17. What will God's Word do in your life? How will these effects of God's Word help you stay close to Jesus?

"You are my friends if you do what I command. I no longer call you servants, because a servant does not know his master's business. Instead, I have called you friends, for everything that I learned from my Father I have made known to you."
John 15:14,15

THE COMPLETE JUNIOR HIGH BIBLE STUDY RESOURCE BOOK #5
© 1988 GL/LIGHT FORCE, VENTURA, CA 93006

THEME: We are members of God's family.

Session 4

BIBLE STUDY OUTLINE

Read Matthew 12:46-50 to your listeners. You can do the Object Lesson before or after you read the Scripture. Make these points as the clock allows:

Verse 46: Jesus was popular with the crowds at this time. He was in demand because He spoke the truth with power and authority. His words were like food to a starving person—and the crowds came to feast. Jesus is the same today. He has words of truth and salvation for those who want to hear. In the back of the crowd, Jesus' family stood, waiting to speak to Him.

Verses 47-49: Jesus never lost an opportunity to make an important point. When someone told Jesus His family awaited, Jesus declared that the real members of His family—His spiritual, Christian family—are those people who do the will of God the Father. There are a couple of important lessons to learn here: It's important to be in God's will; and if we are, we are actual members of God's family. We aren't just followers or slaves or toys for God to play with—we are His very own flesh and blood. But only if we do His will.

NOTES

OBJECT LESSON: FAMILY MEMBERS

Materials needed: three varieties of flowers and two unrelated objects such as a shoe and a cup.

Show all the items to your students. Ask, **Which of these items appear to be related?** The three flowers are related. Allow your students to give reasons why they believe the flowers are related. Some answers may be: they look pretty much alike, they all have petals, they aren't like the other objects.

Explain that the flowers are similar in many respects. They all have the same purpose, they are all members of the plant kingdom, they do indeed look alike. In the same way, members of God's family—people who do His will—are related to God. They are to seek to be like Him, they are members of His kingdom, and they have a God-given purpose for living.

DISCUSSION QUESTIONS

1. **The Bible passage talks about God's will. What are some of the basic things God wants us to do or be to be in His will?**

2. **How can we know when we are in God's will?**

3. **How can we be a part of God's family?**

4. **Why is it important to be a member of God's family?**

5. **What would you say to someone who said he or she will become a Christian after he or she is old and has had all the fun?**

THE COMPLETE
JUNIOR HIGH BIBLE STUDY
RESOURCE BOOK #5

Action games.

SUCKER'S PUNCH

For three or more players. Requires buckets (equal to the number of players). Each bucket requires a garden hose. The hoses must be alike, and the buckets must hold equal amounts of water. The game must be played outdoors or a large basin to catch the water must be provided.

Place the full buckets on the floor or have them slightly elevated. Place one end of a hose in each bucket, and give the other end of each hose to a volunteer. On your signal, players suck on the hoses, attempting to siphon the water out of the buckets. The first player to empty a bucket wins. This can be played in rounds with winners playing winners for the "Biggest Sucker in the West" championships.

BULL'S EYE DODGE BALL

Line up players as in a regular game of dodge ball: everyone against a wall and one player several feet away, standing behind a line on the floor. The player behind the line throws a soccer ball (or similar) at the players against the wall. If a player is hit, he or she must go out of the game. If the player catches the ball, he or she is safe. Of course, the players may try to dodge the ball, but they must not go out of bounds.

The thing that makes this game different is this: a second player holds a large hoop midway between the thrower and the players standing against the wall—the thrower must throw the ball through the hoop as he tries to hit a player. The thrower and the hoop holder are working together to score hits. When everybody is out, you may choose a new thrower and hoop holder to play again.

SENTENCE STRUCTURE

This is a relatively quiet game, good for small groups and relaxed moments.

Seat everyone in a circle. The first player makes up a simple statement and says it aloud to the group. The second player adds a phrase. The players continue taking turns around the circle, each time repeating accurately all that was said before as well as adding something new. The phrases can be added to the beginning, middle or end of the sentence. The resulting sentence can be nonsensical and will probably turn out to be hilarious. Any player who messes up is out.

He Accepts Us

WHAT THE SESSION IS ABOUT

Jesus attributes great worth to people, no matter how little we may think of ourselves.

SCRIPTURE STUDIED

Mark 5:1-20

KEY PASSAGE

"Go home to your family and tell them how much the Lord has done for you, and how he has had mercy on you." Mark 5:19

AIMS OF THE SESSION

During this session your learners will:

1. Analyze the biblical account of the demon-possessed man who was befriended by Jesus;
2. Tell how Jesus' treatment of the demon-possessed man shows how He will treat confused people today;
3. Thank God that He loves them even when they're confused.

INSIGHTS FOR THE LEADER

Your junior highers are often confused. And why not? Dozens of conflicts pull them in all directions at once, in every area of life—physical, social, spiritual, emotional. Some junior highers develop skill at concealing their conflicts behind a "cool," flippant image. Even those who have their lives firmly centered in Christ also have conflicts simply because they are changing from children to adults, from dependence to independence.

Junior high students may be tempted to think that if they can only get all this confusion straightened out, they'll be accepted by God. This session focuses on the truth that Christ loves, understands and accepts them even with all their conflicts and confusion.

Students raised in the church probably remember the account of the man who lived among the tombs and was possessed by a legion of evil spirits (see Mark 5; also recorded in Matthew 8 and Luke 8). The story may stick with them because of the memorable image of the herd of crazed pigs charging into the water. But the pigs are not the stars of this story! The main characters are Jesus and the torn-apart man whom He befriended.

Early in His ministry, Jesus crossed the Sea of Galilee to its Gentile shore on the east. (Differences in the name of the region He visited come from names of three different towns nearby: Gadara, Gerasa, and Gergesa.) It was on this trip that a squall came up which threatened to swamp the boat and terrified even His fishermen disciples. Jesus slept through the storm. When His disciples woke Him asking, "Teacher, don't you care if we drown?" (Mark 4:38). He rebuked the wind and waves, and the storm stopped.

When they reached the opposite shore, they were met by a man who was raging inside as the storm had been raging outside. He "came from the tombs" (Mark 5:2) where he lived—not a cemetery with headstones as we think of tombs, but burial caves in the hillsides.

Right away it was obvious that here was a man in turmoil being torn many ways at once. He ran up to Jesus and worshiped Him. He "fell on his knees in front of him" (Mark 5:6) while at the same time crying out, "What do you want with me? . . . Swear to God that you won't torture me!" (Mark 5:7). The same inner war had made him throw off all outer restraints. People had tried to subdue this man who wanted and needed so desperately to get control of himself, but "he tore the chains apart and broke the irons on his feet" (Mark 5:4). He was miserably unhappy in his demon-controlled state, but could do nothing to win back control over himself.

The man was confused over who and what he was. Was he the person kneeling before Jesus, or was he all the voices inside him? "My name is Legion," he replied, "for we are many" (Mark 5:9). He could not even give a

clear answer of how many people he was! A Roman "legion" was "a complete army of infantry and cavalry, of upwards of 5,000 men." 1 Evidently there were a great many demons troubling the man!

Any respectable person would have avoided this outcast. But Jesus sailed directly to him. That was His only business that day on the other side of the lake. And while the man was practically begging Jesus to leave him, Jesus was getting to the heart of the matter by talking to the spirits that tormented him. The man whom everyone else rejected was of infinite importance to Christ.

Christ commanded the demons to leave. By the time the people of the surrounding countryside came to find out what was happening the man was "sitting there, dressed and in his right mind" (Mark 5:15). Luke 8:35 says that he was "sitting at Jesus' feet." What chains and fetters had not been able to do, Christ had done! Christ had approached the very confused man with love and acceptance. The man was now free—not to run wild, but to be a mature and responsible person.

Your students may have questions about two intriguing and complex issues: demon possession itself and the drowning of the herd of pigs. Some interpreters have attempted to equate demon possession and mental illness. However, Scripture clearly describes the man's affliction as caused by very real and very personal powers of evil. This account gives a graphic picture of the intensity of the struggle between God and Satan. The demons did not come out at Jesus' first command to them, "for He had been saying to him, 'Come out of the man, you unclean spirit!'" (Mark 5:8, NASB).

Ultimately, however, God's power is seen to be greater than these indescribable evil beings. We also see in Jesus' decision to allow the demons to enter the pigs that He placed greater value on one distraught outcast than on an entire herd of animals. This reflects His teaching in Matthew 6, comparing God's view of people and birds: "Are you not much more valuable than they?" (Matt. 6:26).

What does the unhappy man in Mark 5 have to do with your junior high students? The lesson is not meant to imply that your students are demon-possessed! But they have some points of similarity with the man who lived on the far side of the lake.

1. They are pulled by forces they don't understand. The man didn't even know who he was or how many of him there were. That's close to the way your junior highers often feel. "Am I an adult yet?" they ask. "Am I still a little kid? If I'm an adult, why don't my parents trust me? If I'm still a kid, why do I have so many responsibilities?" There is a "legion" of separate voices inside them saying, "Do this!" "No, do that!"

2. They want Jesus and don't want Him at the same time. Some of your most loyal attenders may also be doing their best to show you how uninterested they are. So you wonder, "If they're that turned off by my class, why do they keep coming?" They may be attracted to the Christian faith but not sure they want to commit everything yet.

3. They constantly fight necessary restrictions. Because they are unsure of themselves, junior highers (in their actions) practically beg for restraints and limits, then do everything possible to throw them off. They know they need outward restrictions, but always try to find some way to break them. Parents and teachers often despair at the failure of their outward rules to control junior highers' behavior. "No man could bind him, no, not with chains . . . neither could any man tame him" (Mark 5:3,4, KJV).

4. Jesus does not wait until they are "straightened out" before He will come to them. Christ attributes great worth and importance to your junior highers just as they are, in their most confused and rebellious times. He is not waiting to claim their lives "some day" when they grow up and become mature. He wants them right now with all their conflicts, so His Spirit can work in their young lives and make them the people He wants them to be.

A reminder for you, the teacher: your junior highers learn about Christ's acceptance of them through studying Scripture such as in today's lesson; but they also learn about His acceptance when they see it in you. How important to you are your junior highers, and how can you let them know this week that they are valuable to you?

Footnote
1. W.E. Vine, *An Expository Dictionary of New Testament Words,* London: Oliphants Ltd., 1940, vol. II, p. 329.

SESSION PLAN

BEFORE CLASS BEGINS: Photocopy the Gateway and the Fun Page.

Attention Grabber

ATTENTION GRABBER (3-5 minutes)

Say to students, **Imagine that you were invited to a formal dinner ("formal" means it's not a fast food joint) with the President or Prime Minister tomorrow night. Besides making your travel arrangements, what would you need to do to get ready?**

As students respond write their answers on the chalkboard or overhead. The point here is that, among other things, they would need to get some appropriate clothes, have a haircut or a new hairdo, or have a quick lesson in protocol. In other words, they would want to look acceptable and act in an acceptable manner.

Make a transition to the EXPLORATION by saying, **Today we're going to look at a story about a man who was far from acceptable— and yet Jesus went out of His way to reach out to him in love and to accept him.**

Bible Exploration

EXPLORATION (40-50 minutes)

Step 1 (10 minutes): Working in pairs or individually, the learners are to read Mark 5:1-13 and write answers to the first five items in the "Tales from the Tomb" section of the Gateway.

Step 2 (8 minutes): Read the first five statements from the "Tales from the Tomb" section and ask learners to share their written responses. Ask for specific verses to support answers.

Open up a further discussion of question 3 by asking: **What reasons do we have to think that**

NOTES

this man wouldn't expect anybody to care about him? Why would it have been so hard to care about him?

Step 3 (4-5 minutes): Now have learners read verses 14-20 and find answers to the last three items.

Step 4 (3-5 minutes): Ask learners to share their answers to the last three items.

Open up further discussion of question 7 by asking, **What feelings changed? Why did they change?**

Remind your students that the changes in the man happened after Christ came to him and worked with him. He did not have to get himself straightened out before Christ would visit him.

Step 5 (10-12 minutes): Have students form groups of three to four. Tell them to look at the "Am I Important to God?" section of their worksheet. Say, **You will find situations in which people think God won't accept them because of what they are thinking. Select one situation and decide how you would answer the person based on what we have learned today. Write** your answer on blank paper (or the back of the worksheet). If you have time, select another one and write your answer. Keep going until I call time.

(If you have a small class, let them remain together as one group to work on this assignment.)

Step 6 (5-10 minutes): Reassemble the class and ask groups to report their responses.

Summarize the point of the session by saying, **We have seen how Jesus went out of His way to seek out the demon-possessed man. He didn't tell him to clean up his act before he came to Jesus. Rather, Jesus reached out to him, helped him and healed him. Sometimes we need Jesus to do that for us. We aren't possessed by demons, but there are things that confuse us. We may think that our thoughts and the way we live make us unacceptable to Him. Today's session shows that Jesus will reach out to us no matter what we're like and will say, "I care about you. Let me help you."**

Conclusion and Decision

CONCLUSION (2-5 minutes)

Tell students, **Turn to the "Phone Call from God" section of your Gateway. Create a dialogue that you and God might have about the things that we have explored in class today. Perhaps you just want to tell God thanks for helping straighten out some area in which you were confused. Perhaps you want to tell Him about some area of confusion that you are experiencing right now. The hardest** part about this is that you need to write in how you think God would respond to what you say. If you are stuck, look over the things that you have discovered about Christ's treatment of the demon-possessed man and take your clues from there.

Close in prayer, thanking God that He loves people even when they're confused.

Distribute Fun Page.

THE GATEWAY

Session 5

Tales from the Tomb

Part 1: Read Mark 5:1-13

Write verse numbers and descriptive phrases for the following:

1. Evidence that the man was torn apart inside:

2. Evidence that other people thought he needed restrictions:

3. Evidence that Jesus cared for him:

4. What did he think of himself before meeting Jesus?

5. What did Jesus think of him?

Part 2: Read Mark 5:14-20

6. Evidence that meeting Jesus changed him.

7. What did he think of himself after he met Jesus?

8. What did he think of Jesus?

Am I Important to God?

I'm not good enough.

I've done things that He won't forgive me for.

I can't change what I'm doing.

I have too many doubts.

I tried it, and it didn't work.

My family belongs to another religion.

Phone Call from God

Create a dialogue that you and God might have about the things explored in class today. Perhaps you just want to tell God thanks for helping straighten out some area in which you were confused, or tell Him about something that is confusing you right now.

Don't forget to include God's reply. (Think about Christ's treatment of the demon-possessed man if you get stuck on that one.)

FUN Page!

Session 5

Mirror, Mirror, File:

Mirror, mirror on the wall, who's the fairest one of all?
Well, some are fair and some are fine, but you, kid, you're the last in line.
Mirror, mirror, tell me true, what is there that I can do?
You could fix your body with some jogging, but your face looks like it took a flogging.
OK, Mirror, say it straight, what will make me look more great?
A ton of money and work might do, to make you look like a #2.
Listen, mirror, I need some hope, 'cause with this face I've got to cope.
All beauty will soon fade away, why not work on what's here to stay?
Mirror, mirror, what do you mean? What can make my life serene?
If I were you, I'd take a look into God's most holy Book.
All right, mirror, what, what will I find in this book to give peace of mind?
You'll find the truth about yourself, so take the Bible off the shelf.
But mirror, mirror, what if I see someone I don't want to be?
That is always where you start, to see the condition of your heart.
Mirror, mirror, there must be more, tell me mirror, I implore!
Jesus wants to make you new, starting over, through and through!
Zowie, mirror, that IS Good News, I'll say good-bye to the blues!
Ask Him to control you, kid, or at life's end you'll wish you did.
Mirror, mirror how can I repay? You have shown me the Way.
Thanks kid, thanks a lot, just drop a quarter in the slot.

People are different! Some are fat, some are thin, some are tall, some are short, some are smart—well, the list goes on and on.

The Bible says that God loves *everybody*. But does He really? Does He love dumb people as much as He loves smart people? Does He love "winos" as much as He loves preachers? Most importantly: does He love YOU as much as He loves other people?!? Let's find out. Fill in the questionnaire below to find out just how much

GOD LOVES YOU!

Circle the answer to each question, then add up the points and compare to the scores below.

1. I love my parents

A. A whole lot. 25 pts.
B. So-so. 10 pts.
C. Yech! 0 pts.

2. When it comes to dogs, I

A. Pet them, play with them, feed them. 25 pts.
B. Sneak them all my liver. 10 pts.
C. Run them over with my bike. 0 pts.

3. When a new kid moved in next door, I

A. Made good friends with him (or her). 25 pts.
B. Ignored him (or her). 10 pts.
C. Pushed his (or her) face in. 0 pts.

4. When I found an egg that had fallen from a bird's nest, I

A. Put it carefully back in the nest. 25 pts.
B. Buried it with a short graveside ceremony. 10 pts.
C. Shook the rest of the eggs down and made breakfast. 0 pts.

5. When it comes to homework, I

A. Always do it well and on time. 25 pts.
B. Do it sometimes. 10 pts.
C. Copy from the kid next door. 0 pts.

6. When my parents tell me to wash the dishes, I

A. Leap up, run into the kitchen, and start scrubbing. 25 pts.
B. Stall around until the "Gilligan's Island" rerun is over. 10 pts.
C. Knock over the dinner table and smash all the dishes. 0 pts.

7. I clean up my room

A. Whenever it's messy. 25 pts.
B. Once a month or so. 10 pts.
C. What do you mean clean? 0 pts.

8. When I play sports with others, I

A. Always play fairly and safely. 25 pts.
B. Sometimes cheat or get mad. 10 pts.
C. Punch out the referees. 0 pts.

9. When I grow up, I want to be

A. A fine, honest, hardworking citizen. 25 pts.
B. Retired by age 30. 10 pts.
C. I ain't gonna grow up! 0 pts.

10. If I had one wish, I'd wish

A. For peace and happiness on earth. 25 pts.
B. For a million dollars. 10 pts.
C. That I'd never started this stupid questionnaire! 0 pts.

11. When it comes to God,

A. I Love Him and believe in Him. 25 pts.
B. I try hard to obey Him, but sometimes I blow it. 10 pts.
C. My family and I worship Maya the Shark Goddess. (We are looking for human sacrifices if you know anyone who'd be available.) 0 pts.

12. When I die, I hope people will remember me for my

A. Generosity and kindness. 25 pts.
B. Stunning good looks. 10 pts.
C. When I die I'm taking everybody with me! 0 pts.

■ DAILY NUGGETS ■

Day 1 Read Psalm 22:1,2. Describe a time when you felt like the writer of these verses.

Day 2 Psalm 22:19-21. Rewrite the passage, naming things that you would like deliverance from in your life in place of "dogs," "lions," etc.

Day 3 Psalm 22:22-24. Describe the writer's feelings after he realizes that God does hear him.

Day 4 Psalm 100:1-5. If you could pick one word to tell what this psalm is about, what would it be?

Day 5 Luke 4:14-19. Make a list of the things Christ came to do.

Day 6 Colossians 1:13. Whose kingdom have we been brought into since becoming Christians?

Add up your score and compare it to this list:

0-100 points: God loves you as much as everybody else!

110-200 points: God loves you as much as everybody else!

210-300 points: God loves you as much as everybody else!

God loves you as much as He loves anybody! Even if you're a rotten person. But remember, because He loves you so much, He wants you to be the very best person you can be!

Session 5

THEME: Prayer and self-doubts.

BIBLE STUDY OUTLINE

Read Psalm 22 to your listeners. Underscore the following points as time allows. (You can do the Object Lesson first or later.)

Introductory remarks: The passage is a prayer of David. He was facing enemies and trials, and God had not yet delivered him. This psalm is often referred to in the Gospels regarding Christ's crucifixion. It is a psalm for anyone facing problems.

Verses 1-2: Often, it seems as if God is far away. This is a common feeling, even with people like David.

Verses 3-5: But God is real, He's great and He's there. In the long run, God answers and no one who waits for Him is disappointed.

Verses 6-18: David describes his situation and feelings, starting with "I am a worm" and ending with "They divide my garments . . . and cast lots for my clothes." While these words may not be the exact ones we'd use to describe our own feelings, we certainly can identify with David's frustration and seeming helplessness. When we have troubles and self-doubts, we feel the same way.

Verses 19-21: David prays for God's deliverance. This is the secret to success. God wants to help us, and He wants to hear from us. Develop the habit of prayer.

Verses 22-31: David vows to honor God publicly (a vow he kept) and he then predicts that future generations will continue to find that He is faithful. Those of us who call on Him will also find that He can be trusted to do what He has promised. Sometimes it seems to take Him too long, but He always comes through in the long run.

OBJECT LESSON: THE GIFTS

Point out to your listeners that one big problem many young people face is self-doubt, or a lousy self-image.

We recommend that you describe any feelings of self-doubt you had and how God has changed your feelings over the years. If you are lucky enough to never have had any doubts, try the following object lesson.

Wrap some trash or decayed garbage in a beautiful box with a lovely ribbon. Add a nice greeting card. Now wrap a five dollar bill in a ripped, filthy piece of paper.

During the meeting, offer to give one of the gifts to someone in the audience. Allow him or her to pick either gift. Give the second gift to someone else. Have everyone gather around to watch the opening of the presents. The good gift should be opened first. After both have been opened say something like, **We tend to think good things come in good looking packages. Sometimes this is true and sometimes it is not. We also tend to think that we are better people if we are handsome or beautiful. Beautiful people are better than ugly people. Happily, God does not believe that. He knows it's what is inside a person that counts. ("Man looks at the outward appearance, but the Lord looks at the heart," 1 Samuel 16:7.) If you are feeling doubts about yourself because of your looks, remember that God will bless and honor you if you are beautiful on the inside.**

DISCUSSION QUESTIONS

1. **What advice would you give to someone who was worried about his or her looks?**

2. **What could you do when it seems as if God is not answering your prayers?**

3. **What are things that people do (or don't do) that tend to hinder God's answering their prayers?**

4. **What advice would you give to someone who has given up on God?**

THE COMPLETE
JUNIOR HIGH BIBLE STUDY
RESOURCE BOOK #5

Here's a special idea that's fun and challenging. Make photocopies of the drawing on this page for your students to look at. Let them view the picture for 30 seconds. Then have them turn the picture over. Ask questions based on the picture such as, "What time is it on the watch?" or "Is the person in the white car a man or a woman?" You can conclude this activity by pointing out that just as many of your students failed to observe much of the picture's information, many people fail to see God's involvement in their lives.

Wise Living

WHAT THE SESSION IS ABOUT

We need God's wisdom in order to make the right decisions in life.

SCRIPTURE STUDIED

Psalm 14:1; Proverbs 1:7; 2:6,7; 3:5,6; 14:9; 16:7; 19:8; 29:9,11; Matthew 7:24-29; Romans 1:21,22; 1 Corinthians 10:12; Galatians 6:3; Titus 3:3; James 1:5; 3:13-18.

KEY PASSAGE

"If any of you lacks wisdom, he should ask God, who gives generously to all without finding fault, and it will be given to him."
James 1:5

AIMS OF THE SESSION

During this session your learners will:

1. Describe from Scripture the contrasts between a fool and a wise person;
2. Discuss the differences that God's wisdom can make in a person's life;
3. Select a specific area about which to ask God for wisdom.

INSIGHTS FOR THE LEADER

If confusion about who they are, what values they should hold, and what feelings they should experience is the ailment of typical junior highers, then the wisdom to do the right thing is the needed cure. Unfortunately, it is noticeably lacking in the lives of most people.

Wisdom is not a very popular commodity in the youth world. It is confused with visions of craggy, white-haired old men sitting in brooding silence and occasionally proclaiming a great insight (for those who have the patience to sit around long enough to hear it). Wisdom is equated with age and experience, and does not appear to kids to be attainable or particularly desirable.

The truth of the matter is that wisdom is what all people need, no matter what their age. It is the focal point of maturity, the catalyst for good thinking, the anchor in the swirling current of modern thought.

Your students face the struggle of choosing between the easy route of foolish thinking and the more difficult, thoughtful path of godly wisdom. Their choices will determine how quickly they mature and what kind of dividends they reap as a consequence of their actions.

True Wisdom

True wisdom comes from God. Godly wisdom is frequently contrasted with worldly wisdom, which at best is severely restricted by its limitation to human ability and at worst is foolish and destructive. Godly wisdom is practical and everyday, involving the ability to understand God's truth and apply it to daily life. It is often vividly contrasted in Scripture with its opposite—foolishness.

The biblical picture indicates that everyone is moving toward becoming wise or becoming foolish. There does not appear to be much middle ground. Scripture tells us that true wisdom comes only from God (see Prov. 1:7; 2:6,7) and that it is directly related to how we obey His Word. Proverbs 3:5,6 says, "Lean not on your own understanding; in all your ways acknowledge him, and he will make your paths straight."

In stark contrast, The Bible states, "The fool says in his heart, 'There is no God'" (Ps. 14:1).

The Builders

Our need for God's wisdom is most keenly felt during times of confusion and problems. Jesus graphically described the perils of trusting human wisdom in His story of the wise and foolish builders (see Matt. 7:24-29). The person who hears and puts God's Word into practice has the resources to withstand pressure. This is not a picture of God saying, "If you obey me, I will keep the storm away from you." Rather, we see God promising that by following His way, we will develop a strong enough foundation for our lives that we will be able to stand during crisis.

NOTES

The fool has no one to turn to except himself when he faces difficulty. He has deceived himself into thinking that he is something he is not (see Gal. 6:3) and he will soon tumble because of his blind pride (see 1 Cor. 10:12).

One area of life in which the lack of wisdom can produce great problems is that of self-control. For example, a person who foolishly loses his or her temper illustrates the proverb that says, "A fool gives full vent to his anger" (Prov. 29:11). And this person will probably reap the results of an uncontrolled rage—a black eye, a bad grade, a sore bottom or a week's duty cleaning out the barn. But wisdom produces harmony, as in the remainder of the verse—"but a wise man keeps himself under control" (Prov. 29:11). The Scripture says of a person with godly wisdom, "When a man's ways are pleasing to the Lord, he makes even his enemies live at peace with him" (Prov. 16:7).

Most of your students will probably have no trouble recalling a situation in which they wish that they had used wisdom. Yet the main problem with using wisdom for the junior higher is that its rewards seem too distant, too far in the future. It is far easier for a young person to reach for the instant gratification that foolish behavior offers. Sometimes wisdom doesn't seem like much fun.

While it is true that the type of wisdom described in James 3:17,18, is not instant, it is the destination toward which we are (or should be) moving. James is talking about the kind of wisdom that those who call themselves Christians should pursue when he says, "The wisdom that comes from heaven is first of all pure; then peace-loving, considerate, submissive, full of mercy and good fruit, impartial and sincere. Peacemakers who sow in peace raise a harvest of righteousness" (Jas. 3:17,18). This is a goal that is hard to attain—we need God's help.

James also lists by-products that result from relying on worldly wisdom: "bitter envy and selfish ambition . . . disorder and every evil practice" (Jas. 3:14,16). These by-products take little time to produce, but a lifetime to get rid of once they are firmly rooted.

To pursue foolish living or wise living is a choice that we make. Romans 1:22 tells us that "although they [people] claimed to be wise, they became fools." Paul reminds us of this choice when he says, "At one time we too were foolish, disobedient, deceived and enslaved by all kinds of passions and pleasures. We lived in malice and envy, being hated and hating one another" (Titus 3:3). The way we live hinges on our relationship with Christ and our willingness to follow His practical teaching regarding values and behavior.

Wisdom is available to us. James writes, "If any of you lacks wisdom, he should ask God, who gives generously to all without finding fault, and it will be given to him" (Jas. 1:5). Encourage your students to seek God's help and understanding for every area of their lives so that they might grow in God's wisdom even while they are young.

SESSION PLAN

BEFORE CLASS BEGINS: Photocopy the Gateway and Fun Page.

Attention Grabber

ATTENTION GRABBER (3-5 minutes)

Ask students, **What do you think a "loser" looks like?** As they respond, write their comments on the chalkboard. (Most of their responses will be physical descriptions.)

Then ask, **What do you think a fool looks like?** Again record their answers. Then ask: **In your opinion, what is the difference between a loser and a fool? What would be the opposite of a fool?**

Make a transition by saying something like this:

You can't tell who's a fool just by looking. A fool might be the best-looking person around, if we look only at the surface. So we have to look a bit deeper. Today we are going to take a look at what it is to be truly wise and what it is to be a fool. I'm going to assume that nobody wants to become a fool. But most of us have a lot to learn about becoming wise. That learning process can begin—or continue—today.

Bible Exploration

EXPLORATION (20-35 minutes)

Step 1 (10-15 minutes): Have students form at least two groups of up to four per group. Direct attention to the "Describe-a-Fool/Words of Wisdom" sections of the Gateway. Assign half the groups to work on "Describe-a-Fool" while the rest do "Words of Wisdom." Tell class, **Work together in your groups to look up the Scriptures and label the drawings according to the information you find.**

Step 2 (5-10 minutes): Regain the attention of the class and ask groups to report their findings on three or four of the questions you select. Provide any additional insights needed using materials from INSIGHTS FOR THE LEADER.

Step 3 (5-7 minutes): Lead a class discussion based on the following four questions. Provide added insights as needed using material from INSIGHTS FOR THE LEADER.

NOTES

1. What important differences are there between a fool and a wise person?

2. What are some things that people your age tend to be foolish about?

3. Why might a non-Christian think that living like a wise person is silly?

4. What is so smart about living the way a wise person lives?

Make a transition to the CONCLUSION by saying something like this: **We've discovered something of what the Bible says about foolishness and wisdom. Everybody needs more of God's wisdom—we never get to the point where we know everything. Our conclusion will give you an opportunity to think and pray about an area of your life in which you especially need that wisdom.**

Conclusion and Decision

CONCLUSION (3-5 minutes)

Tell students, **Turn to the "Don't Fool Yourself" section of the Gateway and thoughtfully complete the assignment you find there.**
Close in prayer and distribute the Fun Page.

Note: You'll need some large self-stick labels for the CONCLUSION to the next session, Session 8 (see page 89).

THE GATEWAY

Describe-a-Fool*

* The word *fool* in the Scripture suggests conceit and pride, not mental inferiority—in other words, the guy is not a dummy!

Words of Wisdom

> "If any of you lacks wisdom, he should ask God, who gives generously to all without finding fault, and it will be given to him."
>
> James 1:5

How does this guy deceive himself?
Galatians 6:3

What a fool does in conversation:
Proverbs 29:9,11

What a fool mocks or laughs at:
Proverbs 14:9

What a fool despises:
Proverbs 1:7

What the fool says in his heart:
Psalm 14:1

What are the by-products of worldly wisdom or foolishness?
James 3:13-16

How did this guy become a fool?
Romans 1:21

List the ways a fool lives:
Titus 3:3

This joker thinks he's standing. What might happen to him?
1 Corinthians 10:12

Where does true wisdom come from?
Proverbs 2:6,7

Heavenly wisdom is:
James 3:17

God will direct your path if:
Proverbs 3:5,6

If you really care about yourself what will you do?
Proverbs 19:8

If you lack wisdom in life you should:
James 1:5

What should you do to be able to withstand troubles?
Matthew 7:24-29

What happens to this guy's enemies when he does what is pleasing to the Lord?
Proverbs 16:7

Don't Fool Yourself

Based on the Scriptures you've read, check the box that best describes you.

☐ I tend to fool myself into thinking that people or things will make me happy.

☐ I want to be wise—but I do act foolishly about certain things.

☐ I feel that I'm growing in wisdom all the time.

☐ Sometimes I'm so wise I surprise myself. Other times—well, I surprise myself then too.

Write down one area in which you lean toward foolishness. For example: Attitudes at home or school, self-control of your mouth, eyes, hands, etc.

How about asking God to give you His wisdom in dealing with your problem area? (Make a written request.)

Reason

The Wisdom File:

Case # Proverbs 16:7 and 29:11

My investigation this week involves three suspects:

1. A hardened criminal in murder, arson, stealing, cheating, lying—well, his police record goes on and on. His name is Satan.

2. A typical young girl named Jane.

3. Her typical twin sister Joan.

I witnessed the following incident. Satan approached Jane and said:

HEY, JANE! DID YOU HEAR THE TERRIBLE GOSSIP SAM SNORKLE IS SPREADING ABOUT YOU? GO PUNCH HIM IN THE SNOUT!

GRRR!

Which she did. It was horrible!

POW!

Then Satan approached sister Joan and said:

HEY, JOAN! DID YOU HEAR THE TERRIBLE GOSSIP SAM SNORKLE IS SPREADING ABOUT YOU? GO PUNCH HIM IN THE SNOUT!

?

NO! THE BIBLE SAYS, "A FOOL GIVES FULL VENT TO HIS ANGER, BUT A WISE MAN KEEPS HIMSELF UNDER CONTROL." PROVERBS 29:11, NIV.

"WHEN A MAN'S WAYS ARE PLEASING TO THE LORD, HE MAKES EVEN HIS ENEMIES TO BE AT PEACE WITH HIM." PROVERB 16:7, NASB. **THAT'S WHAT THE BIBLE SAYS AND THAT'S WHAT I'M GONNA DO!**

CURSES! FOILED AGAIN!

Sleuth's comment:

Jane and Joan are alike in many ways. Both look the same, like the same things, and do many of the same things. But there is ONE IMPORTANT EXCEPTION: Joan is wise. She follows the Bible. She lets God be her guide. Seems to me everyone should be like Joan!

What do you become if you never follow God's wisdom in life?

To answer this important question, fold this whole page over so "B" meets "A" like this:

A▶ ◀B

ANYONE WHO DOESN'T FOLLOW THE BIBLE, GOD'S TOOL FOR BUILDING STRONG CHRISTIANS, IS ONE!

A▶ ◀B

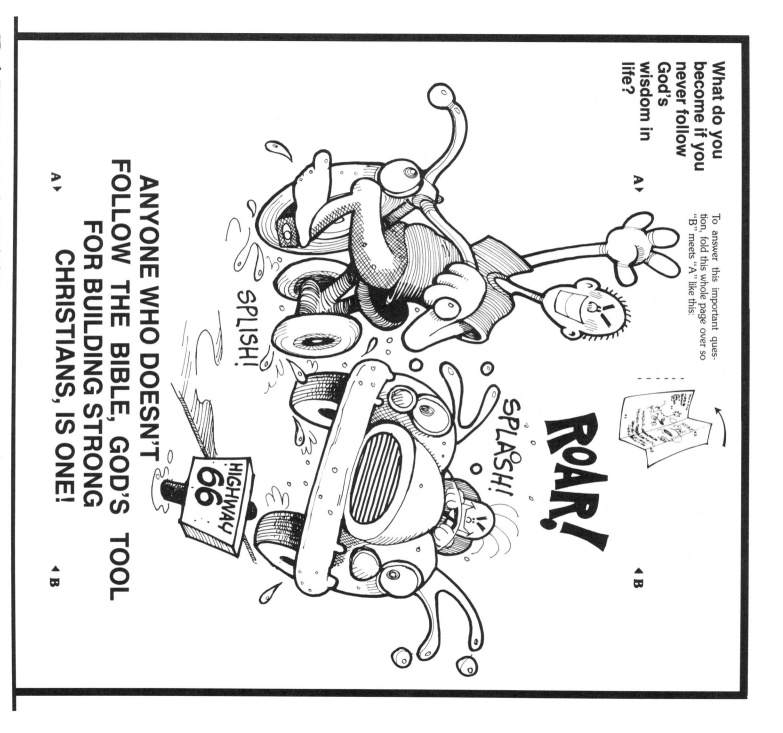

DAILY NUGGETS
Wisdom from God's Word for you to read each day.

Day 1 Read 1 Corinthians 1:18. What is considered foolish by the world?

Day 2 1 Corinthians 1:19-25. What do these verses tell you about man's way of thinking compared to God's?

Day 3 Matthew 7:24-27. Think of an illustration from your everyday life that is similar to this classic example of a fool and a wise man.

Day 4 Luke 12:13-21. In your Bible, circle the sentences or phrases that demonstrate the following steps to foolishness: 1. A fool does not recognize what life consists of. 2. A fool thinks he controls his own destiny. 3. A fool does not take God into consideration.

Day 5 2 Timothy 3:15. According to this verse where can you get the wisdom that leads to salvation?

Day 6 Proverbs 3:5,6. Rewrite this in your own words.

THEME: God's wisdom helps us make smart decisions in life.

Session 6

BIBLE STUDY OUTLINE

Tell the parable of the rich fool (Luke 12:15-21). This same parable was covered in the Session 2 Popsheet of the Junior High Bible Study Resource Book #1, but this lesson approaches the passage from a different angle.

Introductory remarks: Say something like, **We are going to look at a man who was a fool. Let's see what steps he took to become a fool.**

Verses 15-18: In these verses we see no real sign of foolishness. In fact, the man appears to be a pretty sharp guy—he was wealthy, he had productive land and he planned ahead to store the excess crop. In short, he seems to be a wise manager.

Verse 19: Here we see the first sign of his foolishness. He decided to "eat, drink and be merry." But what's wrong with that? Is that so foolish? Not on the surface perhaps—but the underlying motive can be extremely foolish. The sense of the passage is that the man thought that eating, drinking and being merry is the whole point to life—that God has no part in a person's life.

Verses 20,21: God steps in and informs the man that his life is over. Worst of all, Jesus tells us that the man was rich in worldly possessions, but bankrupt toward God. That's the ultimate foolishness. The steps of foolishness are simple: (1) The fool does not recognize what life consists of (not possessions or wealth, but living the way God wants us to). (2) The fool thinks he controls his own destiny (believing there is no God). (3) The fool does not take God into consideration (even if he thinks God exists, he ignores Him).

POEM: TINKER TOY BOYS

Recite this poem to your listeners. You may wish to turn this into an object lesson by showing a toy construction set of some sort.

Once upon a time there were two little boys,
    who loved to play with their little Tinker Toys.
Buildings and bridges and other such joys,
    made the two little boys with their little Tinker Toys.

Both grew older, grew up, became men,
    went their own ways, never met again.
A teacher taught one to build buildings for real,
    the other one played with his Tinker Toys still.

The Bible is a teacher too, so read it each day,
    and when you grow up you'll be able to say:
"God made my life wonderful, full of purpose and joys!"
    And you won't be a fool, playing with toys.

There's a lesson to be learned here, a moral, a rule:
    Be like the wise man, and not like the fool.

DISCUSSION QUESTIONS

1. **What point or points was Jesus trying to make with this parable?**

2. **What does the word fool mean to you? What is the most foolish thing you've ever seen?**

3. **How is it possible to be worldly wise and spiritually foolish?**

4. **How can a spiritually foolish person get on the right track to wisdom?**

THE COMPLETE
JUNIOR HIGH BIBLE STUDY
RESOURCE BOOK #5

Fun with your VCR.

GROUP ANNOUNCEMENTS

This week, do something fun and unique with your announcements. Videotape the announcements in three easy steps:

1. Write your announcements on a sheet of paper. For an example, let's say your announcement is, "Don't forget the Pig Party Friday Night."

2. Assemble a group of volunteers to read the announcement while you tape.

3. Have the first volunteer read the first word ("Don't") into the camera (close up). Then tape the next volunteer as he or she reads the second word ("forget"). Do this until all the words have been read. Be sure to quick cut between takes, so that when the tape is played the faces flash by as the announcement is given.

CANDID TEACHERS

Videotape several of the teachers that your students have in school. Simply tape them (secretly) as they walk on the campus during lunch time. When you show the tape, play background music with a beat. It's a simple event, but usually good for a load of laughs.

WHOSE HOUSE IS THIS?

Tape a "House of the Month" (belonging to one of your students). Object is for your group to guess whose house it is. The clues at first should be very difficult—for example, do a close-up shot of the back wall of a closet. After each clue allow students to hazard a guess.

Abundant Life

INSIGHTS FOR THE LEADER

WHAT THE SESSION IS ABOUT

Christ makes us, His followers, successful from the inside out.

SCRIPTURE STUDIED

Proverbs 16:25; 21:21,30; 22:1,4; 31:30; Ecclesiastes 2:1-11; Matthew 6:19-21,31-33; Ephesians 6:10; James 1:5; 1 John 3:3

KEY PASSAGE

"The thief comes only to steal and kill and destroy; I have come that they may have life, and have it to the full." John 10:10

AIMS OF THE SESSION

During this session your learners will:

1. Examine Scriptures that deal with true success;

2. Compare God's concept of success with the world's;

3. Make a reminder of how they can have God's kind of success.

Nobody wants to be a failure in life. Nobody wants to feel that he or she has nothing to offer or that he or she is not cared for by anyone. No one wants to be at the bottom of the heap. Yet these are often the experiences of junior highers as they enter the adolescent years.

There are few places more merciless than a junior high campus. You can be put on the "out" list for not wearing the right clothes or for not being "into" the right thing. The more fortunate outcasts from the "super-cool" group will band together and form their own group with its own pecking order. The remainder will be left to peer in from the outside, having their worth as human beings questioned over and over again.

Even those who are "in" with a group are not secure. They must constantly prove themselves and must not vary too much from the established order or they will find themselves banned from the crowd.

It is during early adolescence that the need to be a worldly success in life is brought into sharp focus. Success may mean building the prowess of an athlete, the seductiveness of a movie star, the toughness of a convict or the wit of a comedian. When natural talent or skills fail to measure up, success can always be obtained if one has the money, power or connections to do so.

It is into this picture of young people reaching for the golden ring of worldly success that the teachings of Jesus Christ must come. For many teenagers the pattern has been set, the goals and values have been taught by schools, media and often the home. Our students have been programmed into thinking, "If I can just achieve this or that, I will be a success in life."

Jesus sets a different standard of success from the one adopted by the world. The world sets its sights on money, fame, power, beauty, education, or a host of other things to satisfy our need to have others think that we have worth or value.

The Scriptures clearly teach that success comes from a personal relationship with God. The kind of success that really fills the deepest human needs is not found in externals such as possessions or accomplishments. It is measured in terms of what a person becomes internally, in godly character—in the part of a person that lasts through eternity.

Solomon's Failure

King Solomon gives a wonderful example of the futility of trying to pursue personal success by the means recognized by the world. Ecclesiastes 2:1-11 tells us that he tried pleasure—having a good time. He tried artificial stimulants; he tried productivity and collecting material goods; and he tried companionship. He says, "I denied myself nothing my eyes desired; I refused my heart no pleasure.

NOTES

My heart took delight in all my work, and this was the reward for all my labor. Yet when I surveyed all that my hands had done and what I had toiled to achieve, everything was meaningless, a chasing after the wind; nothing was gained under the sun" (Eccles. 2:10,11).

Solomon's fortunes, pleasures and fame failed him because he put his trust in them rather than in God.

In an economy that is built upon the financial climb to success and a preoccupation with beauty and looks, the teaching of the Word stands in stark contrast: "Charm is deceptive, and beauty is fleeting; but a woman who fears the Lord is to be praised," comments the writer of Proverbs 31:30. Jesus taught the same principle regarding the true source of a person's value when He said, "Do not store up for yourselves treasures on earth, where moth and rust destroy, and where thieves break in and steal. But store up for yourselves treasures in heaven" (Matt. 6:19,20).

True success is what we are on the inside. Building our "inside" value requires a transformation of our character by the One who made us. This is not popular thinking. Some students may have a difficult time comprehending how the vital needs that people were created with (to be loved and to have value) can be met by relying on God.

It takes only a little thought to see that Christ wants to build in us a character that will be magnetic to others. A good reputation (Prov. 22:1), purity of life (1 John 3:3), humility (Prov. 22:4), wisdom (Jas. 1:5), and strength (Eph. 6:10) are qualities that a person cannot buy or earn with looks, fame or power. Yet these are qualities that cause a person to have true worth.

The direction of biblical teaching is toward developing people in their inner character and in their relationship with God. This leads to the transformation of their relationships with others. The Bible does not exclude financial success, social prominence or competition, but it establishes a proper framework in which they may exist in the lives of some Christians while being monitored by the Holy Spirit. The lack of these factors, however, clearly does not make a person less valuable to God.

God is more concerned about our lives being truly successful and worthwhile than we are. Through Christ He expressed His intent that we might have abundant life, life overflowing (see John 10:10).

But God does not focus on the outward trappings of prosperity; that is not necessarily His kind of abundant life. Because of this His ideas about success do not always make sense to the world.

Scripture teaches, "He who pursues righteousness and love finds life, prosperity and honor" (Prov. 21:21). Success as a person is God's concern for us. It makes much more sense to cooperate with His plan than to try to devise new ones ourselves.

The guidelines for successful living on the spiritual level as well as the human level are found in the Bible. As people adopt those principles and act on them in daily living, they will experience the benefits God offers in terms of the way they feel about themselves and in their relationship with the Lord.

SESSION PLAN

NOTES

BEFORE CLASS BEGINS: Photocopy the Gateway Student Worksheet, the Teaching Resource pages and the Fun Page. The ALTERNATE ATTENTION GRABBER requires felt markers and a sheet of newsprint. The CONCLUSION requires felt pens and large self-stick labels.

Attention Grabber

ATTENTION GRABBER (3-5 minutes)

Tell students, **On your Gateway find the "How Do They Rate?" section. Look at the pictures and decide how you would rate the people you think are successful. Tell why.**

After students have had time to work, ask for volunteers to report their ideas as you take notes on the chalkboard. Then ask them to state what other people their age would consider success to be. List these concepts as well. Retain the lists.

Make a transition to the next part of the session by saying something like this: **Everybody wants to be a success. Part of our relationship with ourselves—the way we feel about ourselves— has to do with needing to feel that we have value. We want other people to think that we have value and that we have done something worthwhile with our lives. Different people have different ideas about what success is as we have seen from our discussion. Let's look at what the Bible has to say about being a successful person and what it says are false kinds of success.**

ALTERNATE ATTENTION GRABBER (7-10 minutes)

Materials needed: Felt pens in various colors and a large sheet of newsprint.

On the newsprint (or on a chalkboard) write, "What Do You Want from Life?" Provide felt pens (or chalk) and ask students to write their responses below the question. When all students have written something, briefly go over what they have contributed.

Then say, **Getting what we want from life is one way to define success. What are some ideas about success that people your age have?** Allow volunteers to suggest answers. Probe to get the kinds of answers that might be given by young people who do not view life from a biblical framework. List these ideas as well.

When time is up or ideas have stopped flowing, make a transition to the next part of the session by saying something like this: **Just about everybody wants to have success in life and to get what he or she wants from life. Often the things that people say they want from life are money, power or fame. But when you dig deeper, it often turns out that people want these because they think these things will give them happiness and feelings of having value**

NOTES

or worth. People need love, joy, happiness, value and worth in order to feel good about themselves—or, we might say, in order to have a good relationship with themselves. Today we're going to see what God has to say about success in life—about what makes a person truly happy and successful, and what things turn into dead ends if we chase after them.

Bible Exploration

EXPLORATION (30-45 minutes)

Step 1 (8-10 minutes): Lead a discussion based on the "Chasing the Wind" section of the Gateway. (Or have students work on the section in small groups.)

Step 2 (8-10 minutes): Distribute "The Matching Maze" Teaching Resource page. Explain, **Now follow the instructions for "The Matching Maze" to find out what the Scriptures say about what is real success and what is merely wasted effort.** Have students work individually or in pairs.

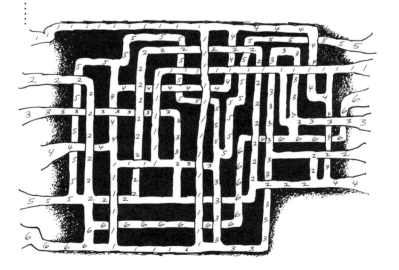

When several students have found the proper solution to the maze reveal the answer to the rest of the class. Discuss the Scripture passages and list on the chalkboard in two columns the things the Bible says will help a person be successful and those that are of no value for real success.

Step 3 (3-4 minutes): Have students form groups. Ask each group to select one item from each of the lists you made in *Step 2*. (Provide some supervision to avoid unnecessary duplication.) Tell students, **Work together in your groups to come up with a reason why having or doing this will or will not make you successful.**

After allowing time for group discussion, ask the students for their ideas. Don't let them get away with one-sentence statements; probe for deeper answers. Use material from INSIGHTS FOR THE LEADER as needed.

Step 4 (3-5 minutes): Direct attention to the list of ideas about success held by people in your students' age group (list was prepared in the ATTENTION GRABBER or the ALTERNATE ATTENTION GRABBER). Do not use the list of students' own ideas about success or what they want from life. Point out the items on the list that correspond with those on the list of biblical concepts of success, and those that correspond with what the Bible says is a waste of time.

Then ask these types of questions: **Why do you think that many people believe being a success in life means getting these things on** the "waste of time" list? Would it be wrong to try to get any of these things? What is the danger of chasing after popularity, wealth or power?

Step 5 (5-8 minutes): Have students return to their original groups. Remind each group of the quality for success that they worked on in Step 3 then say, **Work together in your group to brainstorm ways in which this quality might be displayed in everyday situations. Think about different things that happened at school, at home or in your neighborhood in the last couple of weeks. Did someone display this quality? How did it work out? If no one displayed the quality, how would** things have been different if they had? If you can't think of any events that actually happened, write down some that could happen and tell how your group's quality of success (or lack of success) would show itself in the situation.

Step 6 (5-8 minutes): Reassemble the class and let groups read aloud their results.

Summarize the ideas students have shared. Then make a transition to the Conclusion by saying, **We can see that there is quite a difference between the ideas many people have about success and the ideas God has. Let's take a little time to think about our own views of success and how they compare to God's.**

NOTES

Conclusion and Decision

CONCLUSION (3-5 minutes)

Materials needed: Large self-adhesive labels, felt pens in various colors.

Give each student a self-adhesive label (with its backing still attached) and a felt pen. Explain, **Use the label to make a reminder about the important things we have discovered today about success. You might want to write on your label a slogan such as, "It's not what's on the outside." Or you may write a Scripture verse, a poem, or just a couple of words. If you prefer, draw a picture of what it means to be a true success in life. Then you can take your reminder home and put it on your mirror, your door or someplace else that will bring back to your mind the idea that you want to remember.**

After students have had time to write or draw, allow a few volunteers to share what they have created and what it means.

Close in prayer.

Distribute the Fun Page take-home paper.

THE GATEWAY

"The thief comes only to steal and kill and destroy; I have come that they may have life, and have it to the full."

John 10:10

How Do They Rate?

Look at the people pictured below. Decide how you would rate the people you think are successful, and tell why.

Chasing the Wind

Read Ecclesiastes 2:1-11 (in the Old Testament). Make a list of all the things the writer (King Solomon) achieved or had. What were his feelings after accomplishing and acquiring all this?

What Solomon had:

What were his feelings?

Peek into Proverbs and tell in your own words what is said in these verses:

Proverbs 16:25

Proverbs 21:30

Proverbs 31:30

OK, if all this is just a waste of effort, what are some of the qualities that make a person a true success?

According to Matthew 6:19-21, Jesus tells us to store up treasures where?

How does a person do that?

Check out Matthew 6:31-33. What is the first thing a person should do?

The Matching Maze

The qualities listed on the left side of this page are things that make a person happy, content, joyous and successful on the *inside* (where it really counts). Match the qualities that result from seeking God first with the Scripture (on the right side of the page) that deals with it. Here's how: Look up the passages in your Bible so that you know which verses match with the listed qualities. Then use a pencil to draw lines through the maze to connect the passages with their matching qualities. But: You can't cross your own line (except on paths that obviously pass over or under each other) and you can't use the same section of path twice. Use a pencil with a big eraser!

Qualities:

Bible Passages:

Good name (or reputation)

James 1:5

Proverbs 22:1

Humility

Proverbs 21:21

Pure

1 John 3:3

Steadfast (reliable, steady) or strong

Proverbs 22:4

Ephesians 6:10

Wisdom

Righteousness and honor

What kind of life does Christ want you to have?
See John 10:10

> "The thief comes only to steal and kill and destroy; I have come that they may have life, and have it to the full."
> John 10:10

Hot Hot

Interview: Dave Edwards

Dave Edwards likes to collect snakes and lizards. Don't you? Dave is also a very good songwriter. Concertgoers across America and Europe have enjoyed listening to him and his band. Lately he has become a published author and plans to make writing the focus of his career. We asked him to comment on some important areas in life.

How do you know if you're a success in life?

People have preconceived ideas about what success is, and they live with these all their lives. They start getting programmed during infancy by media, parents and peers. Their ideas about success change as they grow. If they're in grade school, success means a completely different thing than if they're trying to make a living in their thirties.

Would you say most people are successful when they achieve those preconceived ideas of success?

I don't think people know when they are successful. They sometimes are able to reach certain goals, like owning a house or a car, etc. But when they reach these goals they are surprised to learn that they don't FEEL successful.

If you wanted to look back before you die and say, "I've been a success in life," what

would constitute being a success to you?

As a Christian I would say that everything I read in the Bible points me to one place: trying to cooperate with God, in order to be made like Christ.

So you're saying that the closer you walk with God, the more successful you are.

Yes. If He had His way completely, He would make us as much like Christ as possible, without actually being Christ. That's what I get in summary from Scripture. That's the reason we love people, the reason we sing, pray and obey God's commandments. We're transformed from the imperfect into the perfection of Jesus Christ.

Let's talk about heroes. When you were in a more impressionable stage, did you have a hero that you looked up to? Do you have a hero who personifies success?

I definitely don't have the same heroes now that I once had. It's hard to remember specifically someone who was my hero, but I would say it was someone with status.

Status. In what you do as a musician there's status involved. Do people hero-

worship you and others in your line of business?

I think that anyone who is aspiring to a particular profession is going to admire or even idolize the people who have achieved status within that profession. Obviously it's true a lot of the time with music.

When a person idolizes someone, is there a tendency to trust that idol BEYOND the area in which he or she is successful?

I think that always happens. If you follow someone's career, say a baseball player, you begin to feel like you know the person. You feel you can confide in that person. They're in your life. You listen when they tell you what kind of coffee or bicycle to buy.

How can kids monitor their own heroes? How can they know if a particular hero is worthwhile?

The only way to do that is to have a bearing or a standard by which to measure.

And where would you find that?

In the Bible.

DAILY NUGGETS Wisdom from God's Word for you to read each day.

Day 1 Read Matthew 6:19-21. Where should our treasures be stored? How do we do this?

Day 2 Matthew 6:25-27. What does Jesus say about worrying?

Day 3 Matthew 6:28-34. Select and underline the part of this passage that is the most meaningful to you.

Day 4 Philippians 4:6,7. Try writing a short poem on this subject.

Day 5 Proverbs 16:20. What word describes a person who trusts in the Lord?

Day 6 John 10:10. List as many ways as you can think of in which God makes your life different from that of someone who doesn't know Christ.

Sooner or later everyone thinks, "Hey, I want to be a big success in life!" But what is REAL success? A little boy may say to his younger brother or sister, "I want to be a better ball player than you, I hope you drop dead!" A very rich man may say to himself, "I really want to be richer than ever. I'll step on anybody who gets in my way!" A mean girl may cut down her friends just to build herself up. Are these people successful, or are they like cats out on a limb? Will these people fall out of the tree of life? In the circle of success, are they squares?

The television is constantly blasting dumb commercial messages which all say the same thing: "Use our product and you'll be a success!" But is success really this: wearing the latest fashion; gargling with Barfo Mouthwash; wearing Fungus Perfume? NO! Success is not an outer show, putting on a mere mask of respectability.

Instead, it is the inside of a person that counts. It is not so much the outward status symbols as it is the inward peace and joy. In addition, there are two other things the Lord wants you to know. First, God loves you so much He wants you to be successful even more than YOU do! Second, in the end, the ultimate success is being close to God through your relationship with the Lord Jesus Christ.

Your life is too important to waste. Don't be like those sold-out and burned-out people who keep letting the TV tell them that success is driving the newest car or buying the biggest refrigerator.

A successful person is one who is happy and satisfied inside because he keeps his eyes on Him. So take care to remember what success is. Follow the example of Jesus, and don't be like all the rest!

What is the secret of success? Follow the instructions and find out!

1. Cut out all these square-shaped areas.   2. Fold page over to reveal message.

Fold along this line.

THE COMPLETE JUNIOR HIGH BIBLE STUDY RESOURCE BOOK #5
© 1988 GL/LIGHT FORCE, VENTURA, CA 93006

Session 7

THEME: The Pharisee's idea of successful, godly living was different from Christ's.

BIBLE STUDY OUTLINE

Read Matthew 15:1-9 to your students, making these points as time allows:

Verses 1,2: The Pharisees, like many people today, were trying to please God by observing strict rules and regulations (the washing they referred to was ceremonial). It's proper to obey God's laws, but these men were following rules not from the Bible but from their own teachings. Also, they were depending on their own goodness to make them right with God. We know that is impossible—it is grace and faith that count, not good works (see Eph. 2:8,9).

Verses 3-6: Jesus points out the hypocrisy of their position: they break God's laws in order to observe their own.

Verses 7-9: Two important points here: (1) People often are involved in the tragic mistake of honoring God only on the outside, while remaining unchanged on the inside (see v. 8). (2) Living by men's rules, even if ever so sincerely, will not please God. That kind of living is in vain.

Today, we see people who live like Christians on Sunday, but like the devil the rest of the time. God is not at all pleased by this. He wants to change us on the inside—in our behavior, our thinking and our attitudes. Only God's power is strong enough to bring this kind of revolution in a person's life.

OBJECT LESSON:

Bring a piece of veneer wall paneling or some kind of painted object. As students watch, use a sharp knife to scratch off the veneer or paint to reveal the substance once covered. Explain, **This veneer is easily removed to reveal the true nature of this object. Are you a "veneer Christian"—someone who is just a Christian on the surface, but still the same old person inside? God wants real Christians. He wants people who are Christians through and through.**

DISCUSSION QUESTIONS

1. **Why did the Pharisees confront Jesus? What did Jesus try to tell them?**

2. **Do you think the Pharisees responded positively to Jesus' words? What would they—or anyone today—have to do to fulfill what Jesus said?**

3. **Why is it useless to try to get to heaven by good works alone?**

THE COMPLETE
JUNIOR HIGH BIBLE STUDY
RESOURCE BOOK #5

Ideas for Social events.

BABY DINNERS

When a family in your church has a newborn baby, organize volunteers from your youth group into a catering service. Sign up each volunteer to provide a dinner to the family on a specific night. It is then up to the volunteer to contact the family to see what they'd like to eat and to deliver the meal at the appointed time. This is a great gift for a new mom just home from the hospital. One week of delivery service is enough to get most mothers back on their feet.

CHRISTMAS AT SEARS

If your group likes to gather gifts for hospitalized kids or orphans at Christmas time, here is an intelligent way to organize the gift selection.

A few weeks before Christmas take a Sears (or other department store) catalog and a camera (with print film) to where the kids are. Photograph each child individually. Leave the catalog with them, with the instructions that each kid is to pick a toy from the catalog. Limit them to $10.00 per person.

A few days later return to the kids with the developed prints. Have each child write his or her name and gift selection on the back of the appropriate print. (The gifts are identified by catalog page number and item code.)

Make a poster by taping one edge of each photograph to poster board so the photos can be flipped over and information on the back can be read. Hang the poster in your youth group meeting room. Allow each member of the group to pick one child's photograph. The group members then check the catalog, buy the wanted gifts, and wrap them.

On Christmas, throw a party for the children.

A word of warning: Be prepared to buy some gifts if you don't have enough volunteers—and be sure to require 100 percent attendance at the party.

BORN TO SHOP

Have you ever considered taking the shoppers in your group for a day of "malling" in another city? A good way to converse with the kids in your group as you drive along.

Giving of Oneself

WHAT THE SESSION IS ABOUT

My need to be involved with God and other people.

SCRIPTURE STUDIED

Proverbs 3:27; 11:24,25; 14:21; 19:20; 23:12; Matthew 25:34-40; Romans 12:15,16; 1 Thessalonians 3:12; James 1:27

KEY PASSAGE

"One man gives freely, yet gains even more; another withholds unduly, but comes to poverty. A generous man will prosper; he who refreshes others will himself be refreshed." Proverbs 11:24,25

AIMS OF THE SESSION

During this session your learners will:

1. Speculate on what it would be like to be completely alone;
2. Search out what the Bible says about relationships;
3. Respond by making a step to reach out—both giving and receiving.

INSIGHTS FOR THE LEADER

In this session your learners will examine the idea that they have something to offer to other people, and that they can in return receive something from them.

God created people to be in relationships, not to be alone. In fact, after creating Adam God said, "It is not good for the man to be alone" (Gen. 2:18) and promptly created Eve.

The two greatest commandments (see Matt. 22:37-40) are to love God and love one's neighbors—commandments about relationships, not about "going it alone." Paul wrote that the entire law is summed up in love (see Gal. 5:14). He wrote about the church as "the body of Christ" (1 Cor. 12:27) and as "the family of believers" (Gal. 6:10)—terms which express the fact that the members are all essential to one another.

Despite these truths, however, you may find that your students have difficulty in reaching out to others in loving, warm relationships. They are in a difficult period of life, moving between childhood and adulthood. They are growing away from their parents' control and are becoming increasingly independent. They hate to admit dependence on or need for anyone.

They are also unsure of themselves. This encourages them to put up protective walls of self-defense. The sometimes vicious world of the junior high age level also leads them to add bricks and mortar to these walls in order to protect their egos from the battering blows that they would otherwise suffer.

Of course, behind each wall lies an individual to whom God has given potential for much beauty and worth—a person who needs to discover what others can contribute to his or her growth, a person who needs to discover what he or she has to offer to others.

These are not easy tasks for your students. Those who work with junior highers soon discover that the age group is almost all take and no give (with charming exceptions, of course). This session will help open your students' minds to some ideas about what they can give and receive in their relationships with other people and with the Lord.

Giving Categories

This Bible study will give students an opportunity to explore three categories of giving: material giving (money, food, clothing or other tangible goods); emotional giving (compassion, empathy, moral support, enthusiasm); good deeds (helping with practical tasks). The Scriptures to be examined also touch on receiving instruction and advice as examples of the good things one can accept from others in relationships.

Some of the Scriptures may be applied to more than one category, so the following paragraphs will simply deal with the passages one by one in biblical order.

NOTES

"Do not withhold good from those who deserve it, when it is in your power to act" (Prov. 3:27). Here the writer exhorts God's people to provide material or practical help to those who are in need. Notice the realistic provision, "when it is in your power to act." Not everything will be in the power of junior highers, but they should do the things that are. Sharing part of one's lunch with a friend at school or helping Mom by watching the younger kids for a while are examples.

"One man gives freely, yet gains even more; another withholds unduly, but comes to poverty. A generous man will prosper; he who refreshes others will himself be refreshed" (Prov. 11:24,25). Here is a principle that is repeated elsewhere in God's Word: giving to God, either directly or by helping those in need, brings a blessing to the giver. Sometimes this blessing is the joy of seeing the happiness of the person who has received the gift. Sometimes the blessing lies in finding that God has responded by meeting one of the giver's needs. Someone has said, "You can't outgive God." While we do not give in order to get something in return, we do find that when we give we receive blessings.

"He who despises his neighbor sins, but blessed is he who is kind to the needy" (Prov. 14:21). Being kind to the needy begins with providing them with some of the material things they need. It could also mean emotional giving—being warm and compassionate, sharing their joys or providing moral support for their struggle. And it could mean doing good deeds for them, such as repairing a bicycle for a friend who can't afford to pay to have it done or shopping for a neighbor who can't afford a car.

"Listen to advice and accept instruction and in the end you will be wise" (Prov. 19:20). "Apply your heart to instruction and your ears to words of knowledge" (Prov. 23:12). These verses refer to the receiving part of a relationship. Friends can often provide good advice and instruction, which will help a person to become wiser. People who are willing to receive good advice can often save themselves a lot of grief in life by benefiting from the experience and insights of others.

Let's return to the matter of giving. Jesus spoke of a time when rewards would be given to those who had given Him food, drink, hospitality and clothing, had cared for Him in illness and had visited Him in prison. When the people ask when they had done these things for Him, He will reply, "I tell you the truth, whatever you did for one of the least of these brothers of mine, you did for me" (Matt. 25:40). With these words He honored all the practical acts of service and love done in the name of His love throughout the ages. He also provided a list of basic ideas for anyone looking for ways to serve Him. This Scripture covers all three areas of giving: material (food, clothing), emotional (hospitality, visiting the prisoner, caring for the sick), and good deeds (everything on the list).

"Rejoice with those who rejoice; mourn with those who mourn. Live in harmony with one another. Do not be proud, but be willing to associate with people of low position. Do not be conceited" (Rom. 12:15,16). This passage clearly deals with meeting emotional needs. Those who have something to rejoice about need someone who will respond enthusiastically to the news. Those who are in sorrow need someone to help carry that burden. Those who are in a "low position" need to receive the love of Christ as extended to them through people who refuse to be proud and conceited about having a better position in life. Junior highers need to make sure they offer friendship to the less popular people at school and in their neighborhood.

"May the Lord make your love increase and overflow for each other and for everyone else, just as ours does for you" (1 Thess. 3:12). This Scripture fits into the category of emotional help. Everyone needs to be loved. Junior highers can show love by spending time with a friend or family member, by including him or her in plans for activities and outings, by defending him or her when others criticize unfairly, by telling a friend or family member the strengths and good qualities seen in him or her by others, by enthusiastically participating in some of the things that the other person finds important (such as playing a favorite game with a younger brother or sister).

"Religion that God our Father accepts as pure and faultless is this: to look after orphans and widows in their distress and to keep oneself from being polluted by the world" (Jas. 1:27). This final Scripture provides another example of help on all three levels. Looking after orphans and widows will quite often require material help for those who are hard-pressed financially. People can help by giving money or by giving food, clothing and other needed items. Good deeds may also be needed—doing errands and chores that the missing family member used to take care of. And, of course, much emotional giving is needed by people who have lost a loved one. Even after the initial period of shock and mourning has passed, life will never be quite the same. Often people expect someone who has suffered a loss to "get over it" quickly and return to normal. But it isn't so easy to get over a loss like that. People need friends who will continue to listen gladly whenever they feel a need to talk about their situation. These are difficult ideas for junior highers, but if any of your learners are in the sort of situations described you may be able to help them stretch and grow in their maturity.

As your students examine and respond to this session's Scriptures, encourage them to find ways to help other people, and to accept the benefits that can come to them through their relationships with others.

SESSION PLAN

BEFORE CLASS BEGINS: Photocopy the Gateway, Teaching Resource page, and the Fun Page. You'll need scissors for the Teaching Resource game. See the ALTERNATE CONCLUSION for other necessary materials.

Attention Grabber

ATTENTION GRABBER (5-10 minutes)

Tell your students, **Find the pictures of an iceberg and a tropical island on your Gateway. Let's imagine that you were in the first situation of living all alone on an iceberg.** Discuss the questions on the page and any other questions you or your learners think of concerning the effects of living without people in such a physically deprived situation.

Do the same for the tropical island situation. In this case all the person's physical needs would be met, but the person would still be completely deprived of contact with other human beings. What effect would that have on the learner?

Make a transition to the EXPLORATION by saying: **Relationships are a natural and necessary part of our lives. God made us that way. Today we're going to look at some of the things the Bible says about relationships.**

NOTES

ALTERNATE ATTENTION GRABBER
(5-7 minutes)

Before class, write on the chalkboard: "People are important because . . . . " As students arrive, ask them to contribute something to the chalkboard or newsprint by completing the sentence.

When you are ready to begin class say something like, **We have some great ideas listed as to why people are important. Have you ever noticed how some individuals seem to think that they have no use for anyone else? That they act like they can handle everything that comes along and that they don't need anyone—including God? We are going to take a look at some of this kind of thinking today and see what God's Word has to say about it.**

Bible Exploration

EXPLORATION (25-35 minutes)

Step 1 (10-15 minutes): Write the following headings on the chalkboard: Material Giving, Emotional Giving, Good Deeds, Receiving.

With your class look up the following verses, discuss how to summarize each one and decide in which category or categories it fits. Use material from INSIGHTS FOR THE LEADER to help you here. (If time is tight, assemble your class into small groups and assign each group one or two of the passages to work on.)

Proverbs 3:27;
Proverbs 11:24,25;
Proverbs 14:21;
Proverbs 19:20;
Proverbs 23:12;
Matthew 25:34-40;
Romans 12:15,16;
1 Thessalonians 3:12;
James 1:27

Step 2 (15-20 minutes): Tell students, **Get into pairs or trios.** Distribute the Teaching Resource page and scissors (one of each to every small group). **Play the "Puzzling Palz" game. Come up with a list of things that other people contribute to each of your lives. Then list things someone your age could contribute to the lives of others at home, school, church or**

in the neighborhood. After students have had time to work, have each team share two or three ideas as you jot them on a chalkboard.

(If you have a small group of students you may want to keep them together and let them brainstorm the two lists while you record their ideas on chalkboard or newsprint.)

Ask a few questions like these: **Why do you think some people have a hard time giving to others some of the things you listed? Why do you think some people have a hard time** receiving contributions or kindness from others?

Make a transition to the next part of the session by saying, **It is clear from the Scriptures we have examined that people are important and that God did not design us to go it alone. Not interacting with others would make us selfish. Not having people who care about us would be a lonely situation and might cause us to remain immature.**

Conclusion and Decision

CONCLUSION (4-8 minutes)

Tell learners, **Think about an area of your life in which you have been refusing either to help others** (or to give to God), **or to accept help from others** (or from God). **Thoughtfully write a phrase describing those parts of your life in the part of the Gateway that says, "Parts of my life in which I haven't been willing to . . . ."** **Then find the drawing labeled "Reaching Outside Myself." On one of the person's hands write an action you will take to give this week or in the near future, and on the other hand, write an action you will take to receive this week or in the near future.**

Close the class session in prayer.
Distribute the Fun Page.

ALTERNATE CONCLUSION (10-15 minutes)

Materials needed: Large sheets of butcher paper, scissors and felt markers.

Say to your students, **Think about what you can give to others to let them know you value them. Then think of a creative way to express this on a book cover to use in school. You may wish to write a slogan, create a symbol or draw a situation. Use one side of the book cover to express what you can give to other people and the other side to show ways that you can express to others the value that they have to you. Later, you can cut the cover to the exact size of one of your school books.**

Close in prayer.
Distribute the Fun Page.

Note: Index cards and a container are required for the ALTERNATE CONCLUSION to the next session (Session 9). See page 116 for details.

THE GATEWAY

"One man gives freely, yet gains even more; another withholds unduly, but comes to poverty. A generous man will prosper; he who refreshes others will himself be refreshed."
Proverbs 11:24,25

Suppose you lived on an iceberg all alone . . . .

What would you do for food?

How would you keep warm?

What would you do all day?

OK, now suppose you lived in a tropical paradise all alone . . . .

Who would you talk to?

What would you read?

Would you get lonely?

Reaching Outside Myself

Giving and Receiving

Parts of my life in which I haven't been willing to give to others:

Parts of my life in which I haven't been willing to accept from others:

Puzzling Palz

If you carefully cut out these strange people and place them together properly, like a jigsaw puzzle, they will spell the word "PALS." (The letters are formed by spaces between the people.) When you have completed the puzzle, work together in your group to come up with a list of things that other people contribute to your lives. Then list things someone your age could contribute to the lives of others at home, school, church or in the neighborhood. Both lists should have as many things as there are people in this puzzle.

Sharing things with others is a good way to win friends, that's for sure. Luke 6:38 gives an important tip regarding our generosity. You can find out what Luke 6:38 says by looking it up in the Bible—but that would be too easy! Do it the hard way: unscramble the words below (the ones in bold type) to correctly spell out what Jesus said.

"**VEIG**, AND IT **LIWL** BE **EIGNV** TO YOU. A **DOGO** **SEREMAU**, **DSSEERP** **WOND**, **AENKHS** **RHETTEOG** AND **GNUNINR** **EVRO**, **ILWL** BE **DPOEUR** **TOIN** **OUYR** **ALP**. **RFO** **TWHI** THE **UAMEERS** **UYO** **EUS**, IT WILL BE **AUMESEDR** **OT** **UYO**."

DAILY NUGGETS

Day 1 Read Acts 20:35. What could you give to another this week?

Day 2 Ephesians 5:2. What does this verse say that Christ has given for us?

Day 3 Luke 16:19-31. What could the rich man have done for Lazarus? What did the rich man want Lazarus to do for him?

Day 4 John 13:14,15. What is the meaning of the example Christ provided?

Day 5 1 John 2:10. How could a Christian cause another person to stumble or trip up in his or her spiritual life?

Day 6 1 Corinthians 10:24. Whose good should we seek?

"One man gives freely, yet gains even more; another withholds unduly, but comes to poverty. A generous man will prosper; he who refreshes others will himself be refreshed."
Proverbs 11:24,25

THE COMPLETE JUNIOR HIGH BIBLE STUDY RESOURCE BOOK #5
© 1988 GL/LIGHT FORCE, VENTURA, CA 93006

THEME: Giving of oneself.

Session 8

BIBLE STUDY OUTLINE

This lesson is a quick one—just a few minutes. But Christ's message in Luke 6:38 is simple and easily understood. Read it to your students and make these remarks:

Give and it will be given to you: The principle is simple—if you are in the habit of being a generous, giving person, God will respond in like fashion. The opposite is also simple—don't give and you won't receive.

A good measure: God has a great storehouse of riches and blessings. He's not stingy with us if we aren't stingy in our giving.

Pressed down, shaken together and running over, will be poured into your lap: You can't outgive God. He'll make sure that you are taken care of.

For with the measure you use, it will be measured to you: God keeps careful accounts. He will give as you give. If your attitude is one of caring and sharing in large amounts, God will reward you.

OBJECT LESSON: THE BIG SCOOP

Show your students a large bowl piled high with delicious ice cream. (You may wish to make it a "pig trough"—several brightly colored flavors.) As you display another large, empty bowl and a big spoon or scoop, offer to share your ice cream with the first person who raises his or her hand. As the volunteer comes forward, reveal a tiny baby spoon. Use it to scoop a tiny taste of ice cream into the student's bowl. Thank the student and have him or her sit down with the bowl and spoon to eat.

Point out the principle involved: There's giving and then there's giving! That is, it's possible to be a stingy giver. Ask students to tell how they think God would respond to your "generosity."

As a sign of your good nature, fill the student's bowl and give him or her the large spoon. When the lesson is over, perhaps during discussion time, give everyone bowls, spoons and ice cream.

DISCUSSION QUESTIONS

1. **What was your reaction when you saw the stingy amount of ice cream? What was your reaction when the ice cream was passed out for all to enjoy? How does this relate to what God's attitude is toward the act of giving?**

2. **Does God always reward giving? Is His response always immediate?**

3. **How can we be sure God will live up to His end of the bargain?**

THE COMPLETE
JUNIOR HIGH BIBLE STUDY
RESOURCE BOOK #5

Discussion starters for those days you have no time to prepare.

HOLY HOPSCOTCH

Here's a tongue-in-cheek way to get a discussion rolling. A volunteer closes his or her eyes and picks a verse at random by poking a finger into the Bible. Lead a discussion on the verse by asking such questions as "What does this verse mean?" "Is it a command, a promise, or something else?" "How does it apply to us today?"

SCRAMBLED VERSES

Pick one or more verses to scramble—either by scrambling each word or by rearranging the order of the words. Allow small groups to decode the verses, then lead a discussion.

WHAT'S YOUR FAVORITE VERSE?

Ask students to identify their favorite Bible verse, passage or story. Have them explain why they like the ones they do.

Loving the Unlovely SESSION 9

WHAT THE SESSION IS ABOUT

Jesus taught and practiced befriending people in the "out" group.

SCRIPTURE STUDIED

Matthew 5:43-48; 7:12; Luke 19:1-10

KEY PASSAGE

"If you love those who love you, what reward will you get? Are not even the tax collectors doing that? And if you greet only your brothers, what are you doing more than others? Do not even pagans do that?" Matthew 5:46,47

AIMS OF THE SESSION

During this session your learners will:

1. Examine Jesus' teachings and actions regarding befriending outcasts;
2. Discuss ways a Christian should treat those who do not seem to fit in socially;
3. Choose an action to show friendship this week to a person who is on the "outside."

INSIGHTS FOR THE LEADER

Jesus Christ lived by what He taught. We do not find Him saying one thing and doing another. In the Gospels He instructed people to love enemies and outcasts, and He did what He told others to do.

For junior highers the line between "enemies" and "outcasts" tends to blur. Anyone who is on the "outside" is treated like an "enemy." Therefore, this session will apply principles for treatment of enemies and of outcasts to junior highers' treatment of people on the outside of their social circles.

In Matthew 5:47 Jesus questioned the merits of saluting or greeting or speaking to brothers only (meaning not just blood relations but neighbors and people who share a common interest). The customary Jewish salute or greeting is "Shalom!" It is a wish for peace, prosperity, health and well-being. It is actually a prayer for the other person. Jesus was saying that we should wish outsiders well, not ill. His demand is not so much that we try to force ourselves to like certain people, but that we act in a caring way toward people.

The Revolution

Jesus' command to "love your enemies" is one of the most revolutionary aspects of His gospel. Showing concern for the well-being of people who dislike us cuts against all the normal patterns of relationships. Perhaps no single statement of Jesus' has been so universally ignored by multitudes of His followers. Few of His commands have proven to be as hard for people to obey.

Your junior highers have clear ideas about who is in the "in" group and who is "out," even though the membership of each group may change daily. Most likely, your students see their peers in three groups: "our" group where we fit in and are accepted; an elite group of leaders (considered snobs by those on the outside) who won't let anybody into their inner circle; and a group of misfits whom we will never let into our circle. Students probably both resent the "ins" and long to be part of them, while at the same time not realizing that they are treating the "outs" the same way.

This is a complex issue since your junior highers' groupishness is a natural part of their need to belong and to be accepted by peers. As their teacher, you can help open their eyes and their minds to see that others have the same need to belong. Jesus said, "In everything, do to others what you would have them do to you," (Matt. 7:12). In fact, Jesus said that this simple command summed up all the Old Testament law and the teachings of the prophets! If we think we ought to be treated a certain way, then that is the way we should treat others. Our own sense of fairness and right will tell us how other human beings want to be treated.

Jesus illustrated this command on another

NOTES

occasion with the story of the good Samaritan (see Luke 10:25-37). The Samaritan sacrificed his own time, convenience and money to help a person who was part of an enemy ethnic group.

Jesus lived by what He preached. He associated with people at all levels of society, including Samaritans (hated by Jews), women (looked down on by men) and children (see John 4:4-42; Matt. 19:13-15). He touched and healed the most unfortunate outcasts of all—the lepers, whom no one else would touch or even get too close to (see, for example, Mark 1:40-42).

The Hated Tax Man

Your students will take a look at Jesus' treatment of another kind of outcast: a tax collector (see Luke 19:1-10).

In first-century Palestine, tax collectors were nobody's friends but their own—and possibly Rome's. Merchandise transported by land or sea was subject to tolls payable to Roman officials. Collection of the tolls was farmed out to private contractors (sometimes Roman, sometimes Jewish) who paid for the privilege of collecting the tolls in a certain area, and then tried to make a profit. These middlemen employed Jewish people to do the actual collecting down on the street. It is those hired collectors whom the New Testament calls "publicans" or "tax collectors." They charged excessive amounts to keep themselves, their employers and the Roman officials satisfied. Many Jews believed that submitting to Caesar by paying taxes to him was treason against God; others were less rebellious about the taxes but still looked on them as a tribute to a foreign conqueror. The Jewish tax collectors who took part in Rome's excessive taxation system were hated by Jews for two reasons: They had sold their services to the hated foreign occupation forces, and they were robbing their own people in the process.

Zacchaeus was one of these tax collectors—in fact, he was a "chief tax collector and was wealthy" (Luke 19:2). He was also short, so when he wanted to see Jesus he had to climb a tree (see vv. 3,4). Jesus saw him there and said to him, "Zacchaeus, come down immediately. I must stay at your house today"

(v. 5). Zacchaeus came down and "welcomed him gladly" (v. 6). As a result of Jesus' acceptance of this man, Zacchaeus turned his life over to the Lord. He proposed to give half of his possessions to the poor and to repay four times the amount he had gained from cheating anyone. Jesus said, "Today salvation has come to this house" (v. 9).

Jesus did not demand that Zacchaeus become a good, moral person before He would associate with him. And because He visited Zacchaeus publicly, people criticized Jesus saying, "He has gone to be the guest of a 'sinner'" (v. 7). This sort of acceptance by Jesus is what caused Zacchaeus to turn his life over to Jesus and then to begin righting the wrongs he had done.

The Challenge

Jesus' daring kind of love can challenge your junior highers to make friends with people who are shut out at school, in their neighborhoods, possibly even at church. But the first steps should be small and manageable. If you tell your junior highers they must make all the "outsiders" at school into their best friends, they will shrink away! You may need to begin by defining some outsiders your learners can befriend. It's best not to expect them to begin with the dopers, the gang members and the hard core. Rather, encourage them to notice the "nobodies"—those who aren't as attractive, smart, athletic or "cool" as your young people are (or think they are).

Then, when learners plan an act of friendship this week, it should be something they can and will carry out. Planning something huge and being unable to do it would only make a gulf between theoretical Bible study and practical life application. Encourage learners to plan something simple—like sitting next to the selected person at lunch or on the school bus, talking to him or her between classes or walking home after school with someone who lives nearby.

NOTES

SESSION PLAN

BEFORE CLASS BEGINS: Photocopy the Gateway and Fun Page. The ALTERNATE CONCLU-SION requires index cards and a hat or other container.

Attention Grabber

ATTENTION GRABBER (5-7 minutes)

Tell your class, **Please turn to the "But He's Different!" section of the Gateway. Do the puzzle and then answer the questions. Be prepared to share your answers if I should call on you.**

After students have finished the assignment,

allow them to share their responses to the questions.

Make a transition to the next part of the session by saying, **Today we are going to look at what Jesus taught concerning those whom we think are different or on the outside—and people we just don't like, no matter why.**

Bible Exploration

EXPLORATION (25-35 minutes)

Step 1 (10-12 minutes): Ask your students to form groups of three to five and then turn to the "What Did Christ Say to Do . . . ?" section of the Gateway. Ask them to read the Scriptures there and then complete the assignment. When students have finished ask them to share what they have discovered.

Step 2 (10-12 minutes): Direct students to the "What Did Christ Himself Do?" section of the Gateway. Have them form pairs. Tell them, **Read the Scripture and answer the questions. Then, following directions in the "Jericho Journal"**

part of the Gateway, retell the account from the perspective of one of the following:

A Jewish Zealot or super patriot
Zacchaeus's wife
An embarrassed disciple
Zacchaeus himself
After you have finished, you will share your accounts with the rest of us.

Step 3 (5-10 minutes): Ask each pair to come up with a list of at least five things that make people seem to be "unlovable" (such as being considered unattractive or hard to get along with), and at least

115

NOTES

five ways that the kids in their school treat "unlovable" people. Write these on the chalkboard as they are contributed. Then discuss briefly by asking questions such as the following: **Why do you think kids treat others this way? Do you think Christians should be different in the way they treat people who are considered unlovely? In what ways should Christians be different? How can Christians become different?** Jot students' answers on the chalkboard. Remind your learners that believers develop Christlike character—including love for the unlovely—as they grow in Christ, get to know Him better and learn to rely on His strength instead of depending only on their own. It's a process, not an instant transformation.

Make a transition to the next part of the session by saying something like this: **We have seen Christ's teaching and His example. We have discussed how the unlovable are treated in our society. We have talked about how we as Christians should treat those same people. Now let's think about this on a more personal level.**

Conclusion and Decision

CONCLUSION (5-6 minutes)

Direct your students to the "Which Side Are You On?" section of the Gateway. Ask them to prayerfully complete the Gateway. Then close in prayer. If your students are willing, this is a great opportunity for them to pray about specifics, such as, "God, help me show kindness to Marty; help me not to cut him down but to stand up for him and be his friend."

Distribute the Fun Page as students leave.

ALTERNATE CONCLUSION (3-5 minutes)

Materials needed: Index cards, hat or other container.

Give index cards to students and tell them, **I want you to think about the person that you were reminded of a while ago when we were working on the Gateway. Please silently ask God to help you see one thing that you can do this week to be the kind of lover of the unlovely that Jesus is. Think of one word that describes what you can do. Write it on the card and fold your card in half. For instance, if you can think of something to say to the person you may wish to write "Talk," "Kindness" or "Communicate." If you are thinking of a deed you could do you could write "Share" or "Protect." If you are not ready to take this step in your walk with the Lord leave the card blank. Please put your completed cards in this container so that I can pray for you this week. You may include your name if you wish.**

Close in prayer and distribute the Fun Page.

THE GATEWAY

But He's Different!

One of the characters on this page is different from the rest. Can you find him?

Do you think people who you think are weird or different realize that they are?

What do you think it would take for them to be accepted by other people?

What are some things that make a person seem different?

Jericho Journal

Write down what happened when Jesus visited Jericho (see Luke 19:1–10) and your feelings about it from the perspective of one of the following:

A Jewish zealot (a super patriot who hated traitors like tax collectors);

Zacchaeus's wife (if he had one);

An embarrassed disciple (because Jesus was hanging around with nerds again);

Zacchaeus himself.

"If you love those who love you, what reward will you get? Are not even the tax collectors doing that? And if you greet only your brothers, what are you doing more than others? Do not even pagans do that?"

Matthew 5:46,47

What Did Christ Say to Do About Those Who Don't Fit In?

Unscramble the phrases below, then draw a line from each to the proper matching Bible passage. You can read the passages first to get hints for unscrambling.

Matthew 5:43,44	EEEAAPGSNHTNV (3 words)
Matthew 5:45	OOOETTHDRS (3 words)
Matthew 5:46,47	SSNOEBYAMUYO (4 words)
Matthew 5:48	EPREEBFTC (2 words)
Matthew 7:12	OOEEEUILVYRNMS (3 words)

What Did Christ Himself Do?

Read Luke 19:1–10 and jot down what Christ did for the outcast.

Why was Zacchaeus an outcast?

If he hadn't been a tax collector, would people have made fun of him for some other reason?   Why?

Which Side Are You On?

Based on the story you've studied today, which person do you most resemble (in terms of your usual behavior toward outsiders)?

☐ Well, I guess I'm like the Pharisees. I've got a lot of prejudices.

☐ I'm kinda like an embarrassed disciple. I don't really like outcast types even though Jesus does.

☐ I'm more like Zacchaeus—sort of on the outside looking in.

☐ I'm trying to be like Christ.

☐ I want to be like Christ but I'm not sure what to do.

☐ I'm going to show Christ's love towards _____ this week by (use a blank sheet of paper):

FUN! Pagan!

The Leper File:

Case # Luke 17:11-19

No one ever came to visit the colony. Separated from his or her family and friends, a leper lived in loneliness and sadness.

My assignment was to "get the goods" on the disease known as leprosy. Leprosy is an ugly disease. It causes ulcerations on the skin, deformities, loss of toes and fingers. I decided to carefully observe ten leprous men—I kept my distance.

I discovered that the ten men, as with all lepers, were kept in a small area called a "leper colony." The colony was horrible: poverty, disease, humiliation.

LEPER COLONY GO BACK!

Any leper who traveled was never allowed to come close to anyone else. The leper had to shout, "Unclean! Unclean!" when someone approached.

I followed the ten lepers down the road. People would cringe and stand back. Some would yell at the group. Little kids ran in fright or threw rocks. No one came near.

Suddenly I saw a man walking toward the group. He was Jesus! The lepers stood back and then cried for Jesus to help them.

So much for my investigation of leprosy! All the lepers were healed! Oh, well.

To make a long story short, Jesus healed them. They were whole again!

MY HANDS! MY LEGS! I'M HEALED!

Sleuth's comments:

In the entire time I investigated the lepers, only Jesus Christ showed them love. He cared enough to talk to them, to heal them, to save them.

A lot of people TALK about love, but a person who can show love to the UNLOVELY—well, that's LOVE!

Here's a simple puzzle for you to cut out and assemble. We realize you are much too mature to cut out a dumb puzzle (and this IS a dumb puzzle) but if you happen to be so bored even the old "Gilligan's Island" and "Brady Bunch" reruns hold no fascination for you, give it a try. It's a picture of several characters standing in a group. Pick the one who is an outsider.

DAILY NUGGETS

Wisdom from God's Word for you to read each day.

If you were in this poor guy's situation, what would you do to make friends REALLY FAST?

If you were a member of the "insider group" shown here, how would you convince the other members to let the outsider in too? In other words, do you personally know an outsider? What could you do to show love and consideration for that person?

How do you think Jesus would handle the situation?

Day 1 Read 1 Corinthians 1:26-28. What kind of people does God use?

Day 2 James 1:9,10. Rewrite this paradox in your own words.

Day 3 Psalm 147:6. Draw a doodle of this verse.

Day 4 Romans 15:1-3. Make a list of practical ways that you could do what is asked in these verses.

Day 5 Colossians 3:12,13. What should we "clothe" ourselves with?

Day 6 Mark 12:30-33. Make posters of these sayings and hang them in your room.

THE COMPLETE JUNIOR HIGH BIBLE STUDY RESOURCE BOOK #5
© 1988 GL/LIGHT FORCE, VENTURA, CA 93006

THEME: Befriending the outsider.

Session 9

BIBLE STUDY OUTLINE

As time allows, make the following remarks regarding Mark 12:28-31:

Introductory remarks: Say something like, **In this passage Jesus talks about loving God and loving people. I want to focus in on just one aspect of what Christ said and relate it to the important subject of friendship.**

Verse 28: Jesus was always being tested by the religious leaders of the day. That was because He always had profound, thought-provoking things to say. Jesus spoke truth—the kind of truth that changes lives.

Verses 29-31: The main point of Jesus' words is love. Love God and love your neighbor. These two commandments are the most important of all of God's commandments (the Jewish rabbis counted over 600 in God's Word): Love God and love people. In the second command, Jesus said to love our neighbors as ourselves. God wants us to have friends. People belong with people. *At this point, go to the Thought Provoker.*

What does Jesus mean when He says we are to love our neighbors as ourselves? Does that mean we are to have hot flashes and butterflies in the stomach for every person we see on the street? No, Jesus wasn't talking about romantic love. He meant that we are to help others in need, befriend others who have no friends and do what we can to be good friends—in short, do for others what we would want them to do for us.

The opportunities are there. Probably all of us can think of at least one person who needs a friend: a kid in school who doesn't quite fit in; a family member who needs encouragement. We can fulfill God's commandment by being a good friend to these people.

THOUGHT PROVOKER: THINGS THAT BELONG TOGETHER

Ask your students to identify things that always seem to go together. Start off by suggesting bread and butter, salt and pepper and ham and . . . ?

After your students have named several things, point out that people also belong together. Loneliness is not right—people are made to have friends and companionship.

Now return to the Bible Study Outline notes.

DISCUSSION QUESTIONS

1. **What are the qualities of a good friend?**

2. **What are some suggestions for meeting and becoming friends with somebody new?**

3. **What does it mean to love a neighbor as yourself?**

NOTES

Food Games.

FOOD DARTS

At your next banquet or picnic, take instant photos of the food just before it's served. Hang the photos on a board to form a target for kids to throw darts at. Each player gets enough darts to win a meal. Give second chances to those who are unlucky enough to hit the peas three times!

COINS IN THE CAKE

In Canada and elsewhere, coins wrapped in wax paper or foil are inserted into birthday cakes as party favors for the guests. Place the coins in the baked cake just before you frost it.

MASH TRAPS

When serving mashed potatoes cafeteria style, secretly place a mousetrap in the potatoes on two or three plates. When a person digs a fork into the potatoes, the trap is sprung. The results? The most shocked expressions you'll ever see. This is a conference camp favorite.

Family Life

INSIGHTS FOR THE LEADER

WHAT THE SESSION IS ABOUT

Paul's instructions in Ephesians provide practical ways of showing maturity in family relationships.

SCRIPTURE STUDIED

Ephesians 4:1-3,11-16

KEY PASSAGE

"Instead, speaking the truth in love, we will in all things grow up into him who is the Head, that is, Christ." Ephesians 4:15

AIMS OF THE SESSION

During this session your learners will:

1. Name at least three biblical marks of maturity as evidenced in family relationships;

2. Compare common home problems with maturity goals set by Scripture;

3. Decide to show more maturity at home in a specific way.

As they grow toward adulthood and independence, your junior highers want to prove that they are mature enough to handle life and make their own decisions. Meanwhile they may be receiving ambivalent signals from their parents: treated like adults one day and children the next. (Of course some kids act like adults one day and children the next.) A common response of the junior higher is to rebel against family rules and pressures to prove his or her maturity.

Scripture says that a person demonstrates true maturity by showing love and forgiveness, not by anger and rebellion. Paul wrote of gentleness and honesty and bearing with one another "until we all reach unity in the faith and in the knowledge of the Son of God and become mature, attaining to the whole measure of the fullness of Christ" (Ephesians 4:13).

Remember, however, that what is taught in Ephesians goes against many things in the junior higher's nature. The junior high student is more likely to defy his parents than to forgive them. Why? One big reason is that junior highers recognize that they are maturing in a different world from the one their parents knew at a similar age, but they cannot explain the gulf they feel. Meanwhile their parents are perhaps cracking down in an effort to postpone the growing up or because they recognize dangers that their children can't see. Each year about a million kids in North America can't or won't

take the pressure at home and decide to show their "maturity" by making it on their own.

Maturity on the junior high level is often associated with the manner in which one dresses or carries him- or herself (modeled after those whom the student considers sophisticated) or with the amount of experience one has (or claims to have) in particular vices. Often being "macho" is the peak of the junior high boys' maturity standard. Oddly enough, few young teenagers see that nothing looks quite as silly as a 98-pound, pimple-faced kid swaggering around the street corner trying to look like he is God's gift to women and the terror of the local police force at the same time.

Physical development is the gauge by which many junior highers measure maturity. The kids who have experienced the greatest physical development usually have the leadership roles turned over to them in the junior high world. Unfortunately, all the spinach in the world won't put hair on the chest of an eighth grade boy who is not destined to have much there in the first place—or change the figure of a girl programmed to be forever small.

God Loves Junior Highers

God hasn't forgotten junior highers. He has given them guidelines for maturity in the Scriptures.

At home the facades are down. You are known for who you are. There is no one to try

NOTES

to impress. It is where two forces often collide: the will of the parent and the will of the teen.

The home is where a junior higher may really prove whether the independence that he or she is striving for is justified. It is where he or she demonstrates good sense, love and responsibility—or immaturity and self-centered foolishness.

Some Tips from Paul

Paul wrote about some ways to show maturity:

1. Do your best to get along with others (see Eph. 4:2,3). Getting along with others requires an attitude of cooperation and unselfishness that can take the gunpowder out of a lot of potential fireworks at home.

In verse 3, "make every effort" indicates that this is something we have to work at; it doesn't just come naturally. The verse also indicates that unity within God's family is more important than individual rights. But unity is based on love, not force, which means that authority must be administered (by the parent) and responded to (by the teen) in love for the other person. Both teen and parent have a very difficult task which requires the understanding and support of the person on the other side.

2. Use your gifts to build up others (see Eph. 4:11-13). This attitude helps family members focus on, "How can I help?" rather than "What can I get?" It flies in the teeth of the usual teen practice in which it is considered smart to "dig," "chop" or "cut" other people. It calls for a complete reversal of attitudes towards others—which can be accomplished only with the Lord's help.

3. Keep on knowing Christ better (see Eph. 4:13). This is one of the basic tasks of the believer. It is also the only way to grow in getting along with others and building others up, as discussed in the previous paragraph. Furthermore, a junior higher's growth in this area can give Mom and Dad added confidence in their teen's increasing maturity.

4. Be sure of what you believe and don't shift with the fads (see Eph. 4:14). This kind of faith demonstrates that we have values that belong to us and that we are not riding on the coattails of our friends. A mature faith means going beyond childish

understandings gained in Sunday School, developing a strong knowledge of what the Bible really teaches, and knowing how those teachings apply to life situations.

5. Be honest and loving, not devious (see Eph. 4:15). Honesty and trustworthiness are attributes of maturity that will win privileges at home and the respect of parents. The lack of those qualities leads to suspicion on the parents' part and the teen's feeling, "My parents think the worst of me."

6. Do your part to help others (see Eph. 4:16). Doing our part by shouldering our responsibility is not only for the Body of Christ but for the human family as well. The terms and the conditions differ from home to home and some negotiation is often possible, but the general rule is, "If you eat here, live here and sleep here, then you work here." It is a very unpopular rule. But doing our part prepares us for the real world.

If you understand that the scriptural teachings about maturity go against your junior highers' typical reaction to home pressures, you can present the teaching of the New Testament as what it is—a challenge to the junior higher's normal way of life and an honest alternative to battling with parents. Recognize that the areas of maturity outlined in this session do not come easily to junior highers—perhaps not to anyone. But believers are not left to struggle alone with the growth tasks required by the Lord. God Himself supplies the power as believers make the effort to live His way (see Eph. 3:16-21).

SESSION PLAN

BEFORE CLASS BEGINS: Photocopy the Gateway and the Fun Page.

Attention Grabber

ATTENTION GRABBER (3-5 minutes)

Lead the class in a discussion of what maturity is, writing their ideas on the board and trying to draw out their thoughts about what it means to be mature. Don't attempt to get a final definition, because the Scriptures will be your guide in that. Listen to discover whether your students think of maturity as getting privileges, or taking on responsibilities.

Make a transition to the Bible Exploration by saying: **Today we are going to take a look at maturity in the specific area of family relationships. We'll talk about several marks of maturity and we'll deal with common problems people your age face at home. The Bible has some great tips that can help us grow up and enjoy family life.**

Bible Exploration

EXPLORATION (30-35 minutes)

Step 1 (3-5 minutes): Read aloud Ephesians 4:1-3,11-16. Briefly explain that the intervening verses, 4-10, deal with the fact that Christ is one Lord and that all people who believe in Him belong to one faith. At the same time the verses explain that Christ gives many kinds of gifts to His people, as well as mention His coming to earth, dying, rising again and ascending to heaven.

Step 2 (10-15 minutes): Have students form pairs and tell them, **Paul wrote about the characteristics of a person who is really mature in Christ, that is, really grown-up. In** your Gateway section titled "Match Up" these **characteristics have been put into everyday words. Work together to go through the Scriptures again, finding the different marks of a mature person and matching them up with the verse numbers. Some numbers will be used more than once.**

Step 3 (4-6 minutes): Regain the attention of students and ask for volunteers to report their answers. Correct answers are:

B-3   H-2
C-16   I-14
D-11   J-12
E-1   K-2
F-15   L-13

If a learner has a different answer, listen to his or her reasoning. Perhaps the student has seen something in the passage that others overlooked. Show appreciation for your learners' insights.

Step 4 (2 minutes): Have learners complete the statement at the bottom of the Match Up.

Step 5 (8 minutes): Ask volunteers to read their statements. It is very important to listen closely to the learners' struggles at home and not to appear judgmental in your response. They probably feel misunderstood at home, and by being a person who is willing to try to understand, you can open a door of trust with your learners. Using their statements as a basis for discussion ask, **Why are these verses hard to obey? How can we help ourselves obey? What kinds of conflicts can arise? What are our options?** Begin to discuss how a truly mature young person (as Ephesians describes him or her) would act in that conflict.

Make a transition to the Conclusion by saying: **We all have a choice about how we act in these stressful home situations. We can be mature or immature.**

Conclusion and Decision

CONCLUSION (8-10 minutes)

Have students look at the "It Could Happen This Week" section of their Gateway. Say, **What we've read in Ephesians tells us that true maturity is shown by love, forgiveness and taking responsibility—not by fighting and rebelling to get our own way. Sure it's sometimes hard to forgive and try to live at peace with our families. Jesus knows how we feel—remember He had an earthly, human family to live with. He will help you be really mature.** Ask the students to complete the last section of their Gateway.

Reserve several minutes at the end of the session for any learners to voice their concern about upcoming family situations. Pray for each other. Tell the learners that you will be interested to know, next week, what happened.

Distribute the Fun Page.

ALTERNATE CONCLUSION (8-10 minutes)

Tell students, **We have seen some ideas of ways to be more responsible and mature in our behavior at home. Let's try to focus in on some specific things that we can remind ourselves to do in order to create the kind of environment that breeds trust and independence. I'd like you to create a calendar for the rest of the month** (or for the next month if it is close at hand) **and list on it things you can do in order to demonstrate maturity and responsibility at home. For instance, if your job is to take out the trash each day, write that on the calendar. If you have certain chores to do, write them on the calendar. If you do not say thank you to your parents very often write a reminder on your calendar. We will not ask you to share your calendar unless you wish to. You might want to post it someplace where you will see it but the rest of the family will not find it. That way**

it will be a strictly personal reminder.

Allow students to work, then ask for a few volunteers to share their work. Do not press students if they are reluctant.

Close in prayer.

Distribute the Fun Page take-home paper as students leave.

Note: Important advance preparations are required for the next session, Session 11. See BEFORE CLASS BEGINS on page 137 for details.

Your students may wish to see this solution to the Fun Page puzzle.

(If you like, write the solution on an extra copy of the Fun Page and pin it to your classroom bulletin board.)

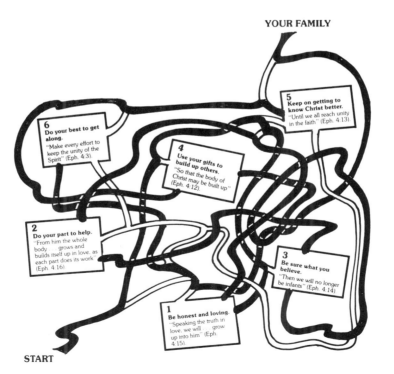

YOUR FAMILY

6 Do your best to get along. "Make every effort to keep the unity of the Spirit" (Eph. 4:3).

5 Keep on getting to know Christ better. "Until we all reach unity in the faith" (Eph. 4:13).

4 Use your gifts to build up others. "So that the body of Christ may be built up" (Eph. 4:12).

2 Do your part to help. "From him the whole body grows and builds itself up in love, as each part does its work" (Eph. 4:16).

3 Be sure what you believe. "Then we will no longer be infants" (Eph. 4:14).

1 Be honest and loving. "Speaking the truth in love, we will grow up into him" (Eph. 4:15).

START

THE GATEWAY

Session 10

Match Up

Read Ephesians 4:1-3,11-16. Then draw a line from each characteristic of a mature Christian to its corresponding verse number. Some numbers are used more than once.

Marks of Maturity

A. I know what I believe; I don't follow every new idea.

B. I want peace at home, not fighting.

C. I pull my own weight; that's how I grow up.

D. I recognize the spiritual leaders God has equipped to help me grow.

E. I want the actions of my life to be like Christ's.

F. I tell my parents the truth and don't sneak around.

G. I respond to the people in my family with love and patience.

H. I try to be patient even when it's hard (which is all the time).

I. I don't act like a baby.

J. I want God to get me ready to serve other people.

K. I don't insist on my own way.

L. I want Christ to be my example.

Verse number

16

15

14

13

12

11

3

2

1

> "Instead, speaking the truth in love, we will in all things grow up into him who is the Head, that is, Christ."
> **Ephesians 4:15**

Complete this Statement:

The hardest verse for me to live at home is _____ because:

It Could Happen This Week

This week I expect this possible family conflict to come up:

I can either (mature reaction):

Or (immature reaction):

I will show my maturity by:

What I expect to happen as a result is:

"Instead, speaking the truth in love, we will in all things grow up into him who is the Head, that is, Christ."
Ephesians 4:15

Interview with: Your Mom and Dad!

Due to the sensitive nature of this interview, your mom and dad are in disguise so they won't be recognized. They will refer to you as "Junior" and use the male gender (he, him) to protect your identity.

The Sleuth: We would like to ask you about your child, Junior.

Dad: Uh, oh, what's he done now?

The Sleuth: Nothing (that we know of). We would just like to hear what you REALLY think about Junior. Things you may never talk to him about.

Mom: That's nice, young man. Would you like some homemade cookies and milk?

The Sleuth: Yeah, sure. Anyway, if there was one thing about Junior you could improve, what would it be?

Mom and Dad: GRATITUDE!

Dad: Junior is so ungrateful for everything we have done for him. He may not be truly ungrateful, but we would never know it.

The Sleuth: What would you want Junior to do?

Mom and Dad: Oh, maybe he could talk to us some, tell us he thinks we're special or something.

Dad: He could think of his mom and go out of his way for her some. Help save her some work and hassle.

Mom: I'd settle for a simple, Thank you.

The Sleuth: What about homework or chores? Do you have strong feelings in these areas?

Dad: Oh, of course it would be nice if Junior did well in school and took responsibility in chores, but I'd trade all of that to know that he really thought of us as people that he loves.

The Sleuth: I'm sure Junior really loves you.

Dad: I guess, but we long to hear him say so!

The Sleuth: Well, junior high kids have a lot on their minds and . . .

Mom: Yes. But they are really no different from anyone else. We are all people with hurts and needs. That's what he doesn't seem to understand.

The Sleuth: Gee, you don't sound like parents to me! You mean you really have feelings?

Dad: That's what we wish Junior realized!

The Sleuth: Well, try to see Junior's point of view. All his life you've been controlling him, making his decisions for him and telling him what to do. Now you want him to thank you for being his boss!

Mom: Hey, who sent you, anyway?

Dad: Yeah, how old are you? We see Junior's point of view, but it's not really correct. We "controlled" him because we love him. We aren't perfect, we make mistakes, but we want him to understand what we are trying to do. When we guide him through life, it's because we want the very best things for him and to save him hurt and pain. We wish he would see that and be grateful—even if he doesn't always agree with us.

The Sleuth: Sounds reasonable. Would you like to say something about the music he listens to, or his flaky friends or his sloppy room?

Mom: No, we think we can work on anything that might be a problem as long as we can open up a channel of communication and mutual appreciation for each other.

The Sleuth: You mean you'll actually LISTEN to your kid? Are you sure you're really real parents?

Mom and Dad: We're sure!

The Family Maze!

It's your job to get close to your family—not just in real life, but in this game, too! As you draw a line from START to YOUR FAMILY, you must enter and pass through the boxes that contain Bible verses. These verses are good tips for staying close to your family (and friends) in real life. The rules: you must draw your line through all boxes and you must do them in proper order (1 to 6). Your lines must not cross (except on paths that obviously pass over and under each other) and you cannot use the same segment of path twice.

START

YOUR FAMILY

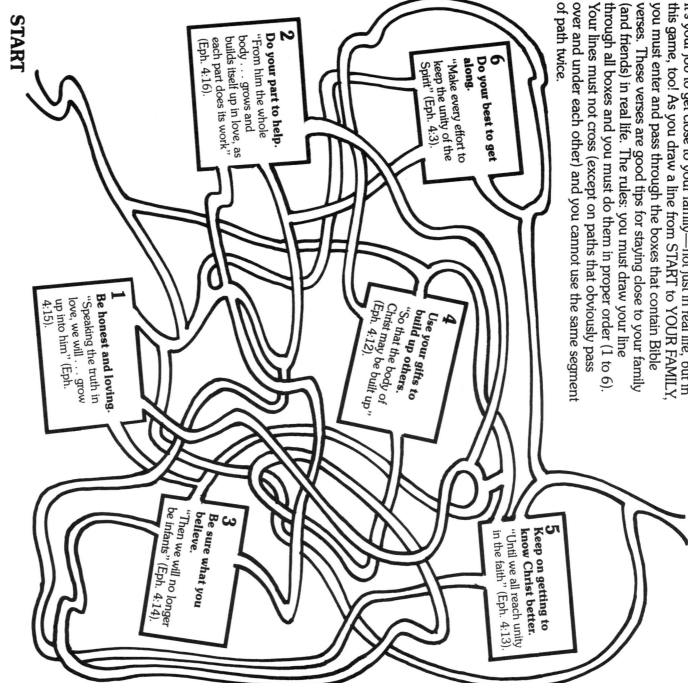

6
Do your best to get along.
"Make every effort to keep the unity of the Spirit" (Eph. 4:3).

2
Do your part to help.
"From him the whole body . . . grows and builds itself up in love, as each part does its work" (Eph. 4:16).

1
Be honest and loving.
"Speaking the truth in love, we will . . . grow up into him" (Eph. 4:15).

4
Use your gifts to build up others.
"So that the body of Christ may be built up" (Eph. 4:12).

3
Be sure what you believe.
"Then we will no longer be infants" (Eph. 4:14).

5
Keep on getting to know Christ better.
"Until we all reach unity in the faith" (Eph. 4:13).

DAILY NUGGETS
wisdom from God's Word for you to read each day.

Day 1 Read John 12:25,26. Write a paragraph telling what Jesus meant by these verses.

Day 2 Psalm 143:10. What does this verse indicate our attitude should be towards God? How would this affect our attitude toward others?

Day 3 Proverbs 10:1. List three ways you can think of to be the type of "son" described in the first half of the verse.

Day 4 Proverbs 10:5. How can this verse apply to your life?

Day 5 Philippians 2:3. How should we consider others?

Day 6 1 Timothy 4:12. In what areas of life should a young believer set an example?

Session 10

THE COMPLETE JUNIOR HIGH BIBLE STUDY RESOURCE BOOK #5
© 1988 GL/LIGHT FORCE, VENTURA, CA 93006

THEME: Family relations

BIBLE STUDY OUTLINE

This lecture is based on one verse, Proverbs 10:1. Read the verse to your listeners (or have a volunteer read) and point out that the verse reminds us that whatever a person's family situation may be, there is a way to handle it wisely and a way to handle it foolishly. Do the Object Lesson.

OBJECT LESSON: HOUSE OF CARDS

Distribute a few decks of playing cards, enough so each group of two or three students can construct a small house of cards.

While students work to build their houses, tell them that building a real home—that is, a good family situation—requires a great deal of time and effort on the part of everyone in the family. To build a house of cards takes concentration and skill, and to build a loving home takes wisdom and work. Like a house of cards, a family that doesn't build support will eventually fall apart.

To give students extra time to build, you may wish to take time to tell of your experiences with your own family. Collect the cards and lead a discussion based on the following questions.

DISCUSSION QUESTIONS

1. Is there such a thing as a perfect family—one that never experiences friction among its members? What are some of the things that cause friction?

2. How can the things that cause friction be eliminated? What could people your age do to help?

3. In addition to reducing friction by not causing problems, there are a lot of positive things anyone can and should do to promote love and respect in a family. What are some of these positive things?

4. If you were parents of teenagers, how do you think you would handle things in your home? Would you be strict? What positive things would you do to make family life more pleasant for your children?

5. Are the things you mentioned practical or too idealistic for a real family? Why do you think so?

6. Why do you suppose God created the family the way He did? He could have made us like some animals that immediately go out on their own without being raised by their parents. Why didn't He make us like that? What purposes do you think He wants the family to fulfill?

7. What is one specific thing you could do in the next couple of days to make a member of your family happy? Think of one thing for each member.

Here's a poster that you can use to build a discussion around.

Church Life

INSIGHTS FOR THE LEADER

WHAT THE SESSION IS ABOUT

The junior high student is an important part of the Body of Christ.

SCRIPTURE STUDIED

1 Corinthians 12:12-27

KEY PASSAGE

"Now you are the body of Christ, and each one of you is a part of it." 1 Corinthians 12:27

AIMS OF THE SESSION

During this session your learners will:

1. Discover that the Bible says that each Christian is an essential member of the Body of Christ;
2. Discuss ways their age group can contribute to the church;
3. Choose ways to join more fully in the church's life.

On the day of Pentecost, when the Holy Spirit came upon the apostles, Peter stood up and boldly announced that here was the fulfillment of Joel's prophecy: "In the last days, God says, I will pour out my Spirit on all people. Your sons and daughters will prophesy, your young men will see visions, your old men will dream dreams. Even on my servants, both men and women, I will pour out my Spirit in those days, and they will prophesy" (Acts 2:17,18). Joel's words, quoted by Peter (see Joel 2:28,29), describe God's Spirit coming upon people of all ages, enabling them to be used by God.

Jesus promised the Holy Spirit to anyone, young or old, who receives Him as Savior (see John 14:16,17). Your junior highers are included in His promise just as surely as elders or deacons or your pastor are included. Your learners have their place in the Body of Christ right now. Depending on your church's policy, they may or may not be enrolled as members. But regardless of whether they are on the membership roll, your students have an important place among Christ's people!

Today's Scripture from 1 Corinthians 12 is about the unity and diversity of the Body of Christ: its "oneness" and its "many-ness." Like the human body, the Body of Christ is one organism. It may be harder for believers to visualize this oneness of the Christian Body than it is to understand the oneness of the human body because the Body of Christ appears to be quite diverse. But in God's eyes and in the reality of spiritual truth, the Body is one. The members are as closely related to one another as the members of an individual human body.

Yet Christ's Body does have its "many-ness" right alongside its oneness, just as the human body does. Our earthly bodies have hands and feet, eyes and ears, hearts and lungs and stomachs. All look different and serve different purposes. Yet each is vitally necessary to the functioning of the whole body. None of us would want to try to live without some part of his or her body. Nor can any part of each of our bodies claim that it doesn't need the other parts.

Similarly, it is a mistake for any Christian to think he or she has no rightful place in the Body: "If the foot should say, 'Because I am not a hand, I do not belong to the body,' it would not for that reason cease to be part of the body" (1 Cor. 12:15). It is equally a mistake for any Christian to imagine that he or she is all-important: "The eye cannot say to the hand, 'I don't need you!'" (12:21).

It is important to remember that God is the one who chooses the arrangement of the members of the Body of Christ, just as He chose the arrangement of our human bodies (see v. 18). Not everybody can be a hand or an eye. All the parts are needed, even those

NOTES

parts that seem insignificant or "less honorable" (see vv. 22-25). One cannot look down on another's position, for God has selected that position. And no one should feel inferior about his or her own role either, but should remember that God has assigned that role and intends to use that person through it.

Anyone who has hurt a bodily part or lost one because of injury or disease will have a particular appreciation for the importance of the body's members to one another. When one part of the body is hurting, the rest of the body tends to favor that part. A person who has had abdominal surgery discovers that even taking a deep breath can make the incision hurt. So the brain tells the rest of the body to be careful, and the other muscles move very cautiously when they move at all, because the whole body tries to avoid the pain that can come from disturbing the injured part.

Similarly, the Lord expects the members of the Church to "have equal concern for each other. If one part suffers, every part suffers with it; if one part is honored, every part rejoices with it" (vv. 25,26). This is the ideal toward which we are all to grow, under the headship of Jesus Christ. No one is to feel self-sufficient and independent of the Body. No one is to feel unneeded and inferior.

Your junior highers probably lean toward the "inferior" side. Perhaps they consider themselves "on hold" in the church until they grow up. They may not see that they have any place in the church right now. It is fair to say that some churches do better than others in making junior highers feel like a part of the Body of Christ.

It will be good, before you teach this session, to talk over with your pastor (or someone else in charge of your church's program) some way your junior highers can participate more fully in the life of your church. It may be a one-time project or a new, continuing activity.

Some Suggestions

Make a banner or other worship aid for the sanctuary.

Form or join church choirs. (Ask your choir director about the minimum age for the "adult" choir; in some churches anyone past sixth grade is welcome.)

Meet people of other age groups (this one takes some work to get kids past the stage of mumbling and looking at their shoes).

Serve a refreshment after a church function.

Serve at a church dinner.

Participate in a church work day.

Read Scripture and offer prayers in worship services.

Plan and present an entire worship service of their own, or a portion of a regular service.

Assist teachers of younger children, or even teach, in Bible schools and Bible clubs.

Visit retirement homes and nursing homes.

Pitch in with someone in the church who needs help with a special project: cleaning up a lawn or shoveling snow for a disabled person, helping with farm work in a rural area. (Yes, that's helping the church, because the church is the people!)

Present a drama illustrating a biblical story or a principle of Christian living.

When adults are giving testimonies or asking for prayer, junior highers can count themselves in by voicing their own testimony or concern, even if it's only a few words. The adults will listen and be proud of their junior highers. They will also be flattered that junior highers trust them.

Pray for adults in the church during your class or other meetings for junior highers.

As you look for ways to involve your students in the total life of the church, try to keep a variety of activities available. Avoid building a total youth program around one type of involvement (such as youth choir), since kids who don't enjoy that activity may become shut off from the rest of the group, and those who are involved may grow up with a very limited concept of ministry.

SESSION PLAN

BEFORE CLASS BEGINS: See the ALTERNATE ATTENTION GRABBER for special instructions. Photocopy the Gateway and the Fun Page. Step 4 of the EXPLORATION describes a tape recording you are to make before the class begins.

Attention Grabber

ATTENTION GRABBER (3-5 minutes)

Distribute the Gateway and have the students individually decipher the coded Bible verse. Ask students to silently raise their hands when they think they have the answer. The correct solution is 1 Corinthians 12:27: "Now you are the body of Christ, and each one of you is a part of it." After several students have raised their hands, ask one to give the answer and how he or she found it. (The verse is not scrambled; the letters are in proper order but the words break in the wrong spots.)

Thank your students and say something like, **This verse, 1 Corinthians 12:27, tells us that each one of us is a member of Christ's Body here on earth. We will spend the rest of our session today learning what that means and how you can be involved in important ways.**

ALTERNATE ATTENTION GRABBER (5-8 minutes)

Write the words to 1 Corinthians 12:27 on a large sheet of card stock or poster board. Cut the cardboard into jigsaw puzzle-like pieces, enough pieces for each of your regular attenders to have one. A few days before class time, mail the pieces to your students, one per student. Enclose a note in each envelope that says something like, "Please bring this with you to this week's Bible study."

When students arrive for class, ask them to assemble the pieces into a complete puzzle. Some of the pieces will probably be missing because some students are absent or forgot to bring their piece of the puzzle.

Make a transition to the EXPLORATION by saying, **The puzzle isn't complete because some pieces are missing. Each piece has an important part in the puzzle. In the same way, you and I are important parts of Christ's Body, the Church. The Church isn't quite whole until each person is doing his or her part as a Christian.** (Read 1 Corinthians 12:27 to the class.)

137

EXPLORATION (30-40 minutes)

Step 1 (10-12 minutes): Read 1 Corinthians 12:12-21 aloud (or have volunteers read segments). Direct learners' attention to the Bible study in their Gateways titled "Fitting into the Body of Christ." Have students work together in threes or fours to complete the study. (Or lead a discussion.)

Step 2 (3-5 minutes): Reassemble the class and ask for reports. Discuss the answers learners have found in the Scriptures.

Step 3 (5-6 minutes): Briefly review 1 Corinthians 12:22-27, pointing out the concern the members of the Body should have for one another. (Use INSIGHTS FOR THE LEADER as needed.) As you move into Steps 4 and 5 and the Conclusion, students need to understand the reasons why believers should be involved in the work of the Church.

Step 4 (5-8 minutes): As noted in BEFORE CLASS BEGINS, you are to make a tape recording to play to your class. During the week, interview as many of the church staff members as is convenient. Each staff member should record a one or two sentence description of his or her job. For extra fun, have the staffers disguise their voices and put their job descriptions in a riddle form. For example, the senior pastor could say, "I shepherd the flock. Who am I?" The building maintenance manager could say, "I keep the place looking great. Guess who I am before it's too late."

Play the recording to your learners, stopping the tape as necessary to allow students to guess the identities of the staff members. Discuss each person's place in the Body of Christ. Be careful to note that some jobs may seem more important than others, but each is essential to the proper functioning of your local church.

Step 5 (8-10 minutes): Now introduce your church's youth minister (if he or she is someone other than yourself). Allow the youth minister to describe many important areas of need in which your students can be involved. (Areas such as inviting friends to church, setting up meeting rooms, leading songs, providing homes for Bible studies and socials, running the sound system and so on.) Allow students to contribute their own ideas. List all suggestions on the chalkboard. Use INSIGHTS FOR THE LEADER for additional thoughts.

Make a transition to the CONCLUSION of the session by saying, **Scripture says that every one of you has an important place in the Church right now, not just years from now when you're an adult. Let's do some work on finding specific ways you can get personally involved.**

Conclusion and Decision

CONCLUSION (3-5 minutes)

Direct attention to the "I'd Like to Help" section of the Gateway and say, **Check your answer** **thoughtfully. I'm going to ask you to hand in your Gateway when you're done so I can see**

what you have said.

Let students work. Then close in prayer and ask students to give you their Gateway sheets. Distribute the Fun Page take-home paper.

After class, read through the Gateway sheets turned in by students. Find ways to use the students who want to serve. Organize a project in which a number of students expressed similar interest. Pass on names of other interested students to church staff and volunteer helpers so they can put the junior highers to work in their areas of interest.

ALTERNATE CONCLUSION
(10-15 minutes)

Tell students, **We're going to work together to plan a letter to a staff member in our fellowship.** (Specify the appropriate person.) **In our letter we will express how you feel as a group about your role in our church. Also, we will offer to do our part as members of the Body of Christ in the specific ways which we have thought of in our groups. We'll all work together to figure out how to word the letter, and then one of us will copy it onto paper and someone else will deliver it.**

Use the chalkboard to record students' ideas until a final form is decided upon. Then select a student with good handwriting to copy the letter onto paper. Also select a volunteer to deliver the finished letter to the appropriate staff member.

Help students remember that the point of the letter is to express to your church's leadership the idea that their junior highers have something to give.

Close in prayer, asking for God's guidance and wisdom in being the part of the Body of Christ He wants your junior highers to be.

Distribute the Fun Page.

For the class member who is to deliver the letter to the appropriate leader, provide assistance in preparing an explanation of the letter's purpose.

Note: You'll need at least one candy bar for the next session's (Session 12) **ATTENTION GRABBER**. See page **149** for more information.

THE GATEWAY

"Now you are the body of Christ, and each one of you is a part of it."
1 Corinthians 12:27

Fitting into the Body of Christ

Decode This Message:

"NO WYO UARETH EBO DY OFCH RISTA NDEACHO NEOFY OUISA PAR TO FIT."

=== **Read 1 Corinthians 12:12–21 and answer these questions.** ===

1. This passage of Scripture is about:

2. Verses 15 and 16 are talking about people who:

3. What do you think the answers are to the questions in verse 17?

4. Who puts the parts of the body where they belong?

5. Why are they put in the places they are?

6. Verse 21 is talking about people who:

7. In one sentence describe the message of this whole Bible passage.

8. You have a part to play in this church right now. ☐ True ☐ False ☐ I'm not sure

I'd Like to Help (I Think)

=== **Check the box that best speaks for you.** ===

☐ I'd like to help my church by giving my services for things I can do.

☐ Not interested, maybe in a couple of years.

☐ Um, I'm new here and uh . . . well . . . um.

☐ I think that I could serve the people (or a person) in my church by:

☐ You can call me or pass on my name to a person who is organizing for a project.

NAME _____

ADDRESS _____

PHONE _____

I'm usually available on _____

Fun Page

Hot Tip

"Now you are the body of Christ, and each one of you is a part of it."

1 Corinthians 12:27

The Brick Pile File: Case #1 Corinthians 12:27

Here's the way it happened. There was a brick wall, see. It was huge! Biggest stone bricks I ever saw. But wait until you hear what happened!

These are the true facts in the case:

The wall held back the pounding ocean surf.

Every brick fit together perfectly to form the mighty wall. Each brick was vitally important to keep that wall strong!

BAM!

But Rick the Brick felt otherwise . . .

I'M JUST A BRICK. . . I DON'T **FIT IN !!**

So, feeling sorry for himself, Rick the Brick left the wall . . .

SNIFF!

Sleuth's comment:

Some Christian people may feel the way Rick the Brick felt about himself: useless, not up to par, not someone that God would want or need! But the Bible indicates that each Christian is an important and necessary part of the "wall," the Christian Body. (See 1 Corinthians chapter 12.)

So don't be a brickhead! God loves you!

WANTED:
Rick the Brick.

Suspect wanted for questioning in connection with: Being an important, involved member of the Christian body.

Description: Can have any appearance: young, old, short, tall, thin, girl, boy ... in fact, anybody can be and should be a contributing and important member of Christ's body!

Distinguishing marks: Loves the Lord, wants to help other Christians, willing to give of self for others.

Aliases: Can have any name imaginable, from John Smith to Penelope Q. Thudgeeker.

Previous record: Before becoming a Christian the suspect was just another blob in the crowd, but now he has purpose in life and joy in his heart!

Convictions: The suspect has several convictions:
1. Believes in Jesus as Lord and Savior.
2. Desires to serve the Lord any way he can.
3. Knows that every Christian has the same privilege and responsibility he has: to serve the Lord by serving others!

DAILY NUGGETS

Day 1 Read 1 Corinthians 12:4-6. Who is the same through all the "differences" mentioned in these verses?

Day 2 1 Corinthians 12:12,13. Write a summary statement explaining what is said in these verses.

Day 3 1 Corinthians 12:14-19. Create a list of various "parts" or rules that people might be fulfilling in your church.

Day 4 1 Corinthians 12:15-26. How should different people in the church treat each other?

Day 5 1 Corinthians 12:27-31. Who is the "body" of Christ? List some abilities that God has given to people in His Body.

Day 6 1 Corinthians 13:1-3. What is the ultimate gift one Christian can give to another Christian?

THE COMPLETE JUNIOR HIGH BIBLE STUDY RESOURCE BOOK #5
© 1988 GL/LIGHT FORCE, VENTURA, CA 93006

THEME: Areas of service in the youth group.

BIBLE STUDY OUTLINE

Read Acts 2:42-47. Make the following remarks as time permits.

Introductory remarks: This passage describes the early church, right after Jesus ascended into heaven. From it, we can learn a bit about our own group here.

Verse 42: The early Christians were students. They listened to the apostle's teachings, which are now recorded for us in the Bible. They fellowshipped, which means they hung out together and cared for each other. They shared their meals and spent time together in prayer. The key word in this verse is *devoted*. The early Christians were healthy spiritually because they were sold out to Jesus Christ and to each other. Every individual was in some way involved in the local group. That's the key to a healthy church. When each member is contributing, our own youth group is strong.

Verse 43: The Spirit of God was obviously present. When people believe in God and expect Him to work in miraculous ways, He does. His presence is necessary to our group's spiritual health. Notice that God was doing His work through people. God wants to use each of us today.

Verses 44-46: The early Christians were excited about God. They honored Him by meeting together, sharing, meeting each other's needs and eating together. That sort of experience lasted a relatively short time in the early church—soon God spread them around the world to spread the gospel. Today our group exists because of their success at spreading the gospel. These things they did are also things that we can be involved in.

Verse 47: They continued to praise the Lord and they enjoyed the favor of the people in the area. And why not? Good things were happening, and they were happening because each individual was devoted to serving God by service to others. Because of their attitude and devotion, people were joining the group in large numbers.

OBJECT LESSON: BALANCED DIET

Bring in some canned or packaged foods that together represent a good balanced diet: meats, vegetables, fruit, cereals, liquids and so on. Point out (or ask your listeners to explain) what would happen to someone who continually left any of the important food groups out of his or her diet. That person would be unhealthy.

Explain that when all the members of the youth group are actively involved with God and with the group, the group is like a healthy, well-balanced meal. But if some of the members aren't contributing properly, the group suffers. Everyone must be involved, that's the way God wants it to be.

DISCUSSION QUESTIONS

1. **What are some areas of service or experiences our youth group provides for its members?**

2. **What additional opportunities should we provide?**

3. **How can we motivate more members to come to the meetings? How can we help everyone develop a closer relationship with God and with each other?**

4. **Why do you suppose the early Christians were so excited about God? How can we become more like them?**

Action games—for your own specialized Olympiad.

You can create your own Olympic games party by doing tongue-in-cheek versions of the standard events. Dream up your own summer or winter games, similar to the suggestions on this page.

BROOM JAVELIN

Broom Javelin is exactly what it sounds like. Contestants throw brooms for distance. Each contestant plays three rounds.

FRISBEE DISCUS

Frisbee Discus can also be played for distance, but it's more fun to go for accuracy. Create a target with a sheet or towel.

BROKEN BICYCLE RACES

Contestants race up a slight hill by pushing bicycles as shown (pedals can't be used). The hill prevents coasting.

Respect for Others SESSION 12

INSIGHTS FOR THE LEADER

WHAT THE SESSION IS ABOUT

Christian freedom respects other people and does not use them for selfish reasons.

SCRIPTURE STUDIED

Galatians 5:13-18

KEY PASSAGE

"Do not use your freedom to indulge the sinful nature; rather, serve one another in love."
Galatians 5:13

AIMS OF THE SESSION

During this session your learners will:
1. Examine biblical teaching on loving rather than using other people;
2. Talk about ways teens use other people and what God would have them do instead;
3. Write their thoughts about ways to treat others with respect.

The Giving Life

Living a "giving" kind of life takes inner security. We must have our feet firmly planted on our worth and acceptance in Christ in order to take the risk of reaching out to others.

But your junior highers are going through a time of great insecurity, uncertainty and fear. They aren't sure who they are, so they protect themselves in self-centeredness.

Maybe you've noticed how skillful your learners are at cutting each other down. Have you noticed them making fun of someone who can't find the right place in the Bible? Do they ever make not-so-complimentary remarks about a student who isn't there—or even one who is? Some days it seems that their whole nature is selfish.

You're right; it is. In fact, every human being's nature is selfish. "All we like sheep have gone astray; we have turned every one to his own way" (Isa. 53:6, *KJV*). Being self-centered is man's basic problem—though you may think your junior highers are working on it overtime!

Junior highers may apply this self-centeredness to a variety of situations. It may lead them to think of their growing sexual interest in terms of conquest or status. They may feel pressure to live up to a fantasy standard set by the media. They may mistake lust for love. Those who allow themselves to be used may be seeking attention in any form they can find it.

Some may seek to have a little fun at the expense of a weaker member of their age group or in vandalism and general lack of concern for the property of others. They may demonstrate their lack of concern for anyone but themselves by the manner in which they treat their parents or siblings.

Today's Scripture tells us to "serve one another in love" (Gal. 5:13). Love has no room for the selfish using of another person to please only ourselves. Love thinks of the other person first, after the example of Christ. "Each of us should please his neighbor for his good, to build him up. For even Christ did not please himself" (Rom. 15:2,3).

The word "flesh" used in some versions of Galatians 5:13 means humanity's sinful nature, which means self-centeredness. The word is also used to mean the substance of the human body, but often in the New Testament it refers to humanity's unregenerate nature. Don't let "flesh" mislead your junior highers into thinking that the Bible says their bodies are evil. It is the selfish, sinful nature which this Scripture is calling on us not to indulge.

If They Ask About Sex

Feel free to pursue the areas about which your learners have questions. Be a good listener; hear what they are really saying. Try to

NOTES

communicate that sex is not bad or dirty, but that it can be surrounded by wrong conditions. Be sure to spell out God's conditions for enjoyment of His gift (marriage), and to give an explanation of why God wants us to play by His rules.

Galatians 5:13-15 speaks of treating one another in a loving way. Help learners see how this applies to male-female relationships. God's principle is that Christians should think of the other person, not themselves, first. We are to live in love, not self-indulgence. "Love your neighbor as yourself" sums up the entire Jewish Law (it is from Lev. 19:18). It means the same as Matthew 7:12 (see Session 9), "In everything, do to others what you would have them do to you," which Jesus said summed up all the Law and the Prophets. It means that since we don't want others to treat us like things and use us, then we should not treat others that way.

Sharp junior highers may ask what's wrong with sex, then, if both people are enjoying it? Share with them the following points:

1. Sex is more than intercourse; it involves our identity as human beings and all the various ways we have of relating to people.

2. Sex is not wrong intrinsically—in fact, it is God's creation and His gift to the human race. But it is wrong when misused.

3. Having intercourse before marriage means giving oneself totally on the physical level, without being totally committed through marriage. This divides the personality and splits something that God intended to be kept whole. Commitment is not an emotion, it is an action. Total commitment is marriage.

4. Heavy petting leaves an unforgettable impression on the mind. Although it may be momentarily fun, it can foul up for years a person's ability to participate in a committed relationship. The person may be comparing past partners, suffering guilt feelings or may have developed habits of haste and secrecy that are inappropriate in a marriage.

5. Experimenting with sex for self-gratification sets up a pattern which makes it increasingly difficult to learn to use sex to convey love in a meaningful relationship. The high degree of promiscuity in our

society is traceable to a view of sex as gratification. With this sort of attitude, it takes more and more "experiences" to try to find satisfaction—which actually comes only in the context of a loving marriage.

What, then, is the correct response to the pressure for sexual experimentation? The answer is: "Live by the Spirit, and you will not gratify the desires of the sinful nature. For the sinful nature desires what is contrary to the Spirit, and the Spirit what is contrary to the sinful nature. They are in conflict with each other, so that you do not do what you want. But if you are led by the Spirit, you are not under law" (Gal. 5:16-18).

Believers need to understand that there is war between the Spirit of God and the sinful nature that we carry with us. The more we give in to the sinful nature, the stronger it will become. The more we give in to the direction of the Spirit, the stronger His influence in our lives will become. "Walking in the Spirit" means doing what the Spirit urges us to do. We find out what He is urging us to do in several ways:

1. Reading the Bible. All of God's basic instructions for living the Christian life are in His Book. There's no point in asking for special information about a situation that is clearly covered by Scripture: We already have His instructions. (In other words, since premarital sex is already prohibited in the Bible, there's no point in asking for special instructions about it or for God's permission to do it "because the circumstances are so unusual." There are no circumstances in which premarital sex is acceptable, according to Scripture.)

2. Understanding and applying biblical principles. Some situations are not spelled out with specific instructions in God's Word. However, there is usually a principle which can be applied. For example, there are no detailed descriptions for "how far" a couple can go. There is a specific command against fornication (premarital sex). But any action short of that will have to be subjected to scriptural principles such as loving the other person as you love yourself, and doing everything in the name of Christ.

3. If there is no specific command and if there doesn't seem to be an applicable principle, then the person can pray for guidance.

Guidance can come in several ways. One is a direct sense that God is pointing you in a certain direction. Another is through the help of trusted advisors such as a youth worker, pastor or parent. Yet another is prayerfully doing what seems best according to your own ability to understand the situation and the consequences of the various options open to you. (Remember, this is a situation in which there are no clear commands or principles from the Bible to point the way.)

Once we know what the Spirit is urging us to do, the next step is to do it! This is often easier said than done, but God does provide the power (see Eph. 3:16). We have to cooperate with Him and make the effort from our side, but He does not leave us to struggle alone.

Young people who want to live God's way, rather than using other people, need to keep close to the Savior so they can grow to be like Him. They need to walk in the Spirit and ask for His help when obedience comes hard. They need the prayers and living examples of adults around them—including teachers!

SESSION PLAN

BEFORE CLASS BEGINS: Photocopy the Gateway and Fun Page. See the ATTENTION GRABBER for necessary materials.

Attention Grabber

ATTENTION GRABBER (4-6 minutes)

Materials needed: One candy bar in its wrapper. (You may wish to buy candy bars or other treats for the entire class.)

Give the candy bar to one of the learners (not one who's weight conscious!) and tell him or her to unwrap it and eat it. Don't say anything while the person is eating. (Expect some laughter from the others—and jealousy!) Then retrieve the torn wrapper. Ask the student how much he or she cared about how the poor candy bar felt while it was being chewed and swallowed. Discuss why nobody cares about a candy bar's feelings.

Have learners complete the "Candy Bars" section of their Gateway worksheets. Then make a transition to the EXPLORATION by saying, **Do you think people your age sometimes treat each other the way they treat candy bars—they use the other person for their own pleasure without regard for that person?** (Discuss this if the students seem immediately open to it before going on to the next part of the session.) If you like, hand out candy bars or other treats for everyone to enjoy.

Bible Exploration

EXPLORATION (30-40 minutes)

Step 1 (2-3 minutes): Read Galatians 5:13-15 together. Explain (since you may still have learners who don't understand that some New Testament books are letters) that the apostle Paul wrote this letter to Christians in Galatia, an area in what is now Turkey.

Step 2 (5-7 minutes): Ask learners to write answers to "What are some ways people use each other?" on their Gateway sheets. When learners have written for several minutes, ask for some answers. Write them on the board and discuss them. If your students have trouble thinking of specifics, mention some suggestions such as: Picking on the unpopular kids; trying to get a date with the basketball star because it will help your image; copying somebody else's schoolwork; lying, deceiving, misleading others in any way; stealing; cutting down others; going on a date so you can make out with the person; getting somebody else to cover for you while you break school rules or parents' rules.

Step 3 (5-7 minutes): Ask students to write answers to the question "How do people feel when they have been used?" When learners have written for several minutes, ask for some answers. Write them on the board and discuss them.

Since junior highers so regularly treat each other thoughtlessly, many of your students may have painful memories of feeling used. They may have served as the flunkie to unknowingly help someone else break school rules. Perhaps the person in the next desk at school copies their test papers and gets away with it. Popular young people might make cruel jokes at the expense of less-glamorous classmates. This discussion helps those learners express their feelings. It also helps learners who are on the using end understand how others feel about being used.

Sex is likely to be an issue in this discussion. For many (maybe all) of your junior highers, sex is a preoccupation and a source of curiosity and bewilderment. They may feel all of the following: excited, confused, embarrassed, guilty, full of anticipation, scared to death. They are also probably not accustomed to talking about these things at church. Be glad (not shocked) if they are open and honest with you and each other.

The junior higher's natural and God-given awakening to sex is real, but it is also immature. It tends to center around his or her own feelings rather than what is best for another person. Your discussion in this step helps the learner to think about how it feels to be an "object."

Step 4 (8-10 minutes): Read Galatians 5:13-15 again to your group. Discuss what this Scripture passage has to do with dating and boyfriend-girlfriend relationships. Ask questions like the following:

What is wrong with using somebody if both people are enjoying it?

Other than sex, how can a person be used in a boyfriend/girlfriend relationship?

What feelings do you have when you have been used?

What kind of reputation do you think people have who use other people?

What kind of reputation do you think people have who let themselves be used?

If people who use others are selfish, what is the reason that some people allow themselves to be used?

Why do some people keep "score" with others about the people that they have used?

Step 5 (8-10 minutes): Tell students, **Suppose the Galatian church was made up of 100 percent junior highers—what would it be like? Let your imaginations play with that idea. Reread Galatians 5:13-15. Then rewrite it in your own words as though Paul had been writing just for people your age.**

Step 6 (2-3 minutes): Briefly share with students the importance of walking in the Spirit as described in Galatians 5:16-18 (see INSIGHTS FOR THE LEADER for information to use here).

Conclusion and Decision

CONCLUSION (8-10 minutes)

Have students work the "Wrap It Up" assignment on the Gateway. Allow several volunteers to show their work to the rest of the class.

Close in prayer and distribute the Fun Page take-home paper.

Note: The final session, Session 13, is a special review game. Be sure to test the game in advance to be sure you can explain the rules to your students.

Candy Bars

Draw a picture of your favorite candy bar.

When I get hold of a _____ (my favorite candy bar) I:

> "Do not use your freedom to indulge the sinful nature; rather, serve one another in love."
> **Galatians 5:13**

- ☐ Save it;
- ☐ Ask it how it feels today;
- ☐ Bury it;
- ☐ Sing to it;
- ☐ Talk to it about life;
- ☐ Take it to church;
- ☐ Consume it.

What are some ways people use each other?

How do people feel when they have been used?

Suppose the Galatian church were made up of 100 percent junior highers!

If Paul had written Galatians 5:13-15 just for junior high students, I think he would have written it this way:

Wrap It Up

On a blank sheet of paper, design a fancy wrapper for an imaginary candy bar. On the wrapper's "list of ingredients," list at least five good things that you could do to show that you respect and truly care for someone. Also give your candy bar a name and slogan, such as "Yernotta Candy Bar—I'll Treat You Right!"

Interview with your friends!

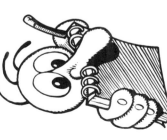

The following is part of an actual interview with a group of students about a very sensitive subject: using people and being used. To gain this candid interview, the Sleuth ventured to great heights (namely, a Christian camp in the mountains), braved icy snow, sun and skiers, and managed to live to tell about it. Names have been changed to protect the innocent, the idiotic and the embarrassed.

Sleuth: How does it make you feel when you realize that you've been used?

Jennifer: Very indecent; you feel really mistreated. Especially when you love somebody, it hurts. It's painful.

Tom: You just feel like nobody wants you, nobody cares, you're worthless. It's a deep feeling.

Mack: Revenge, anger, low.

Sleuth: Low?

Mack: Never come out of your room again, shave your head.

Ken: You feel like it's the end of the world.

Patti: Alone, hurt, mistreated, betrayed, you don't trust them.

Sleuth: How does that make you feel toward other people who haven't used you?

Kathy: You don't trust them.

Sleuth: Have you ever consciously used somebody?

All: Yes.

Sleuth: Uh, um—If it's not too personal, how?

Linda: By using another guy. Say you have a boyfriend and you get into a fight. You go out with his best friend to get to him. You're using the friend; you don't really have any interest in him.

Bob: Yeah. I'd just gotten back from summer camp and I was really "on fire for the Lord." But I took a big fall. I saw this girl at another camp. It was an adult camp and we were bored; we didn't know what to do. I started to mess around with this girl. I felt awful afterwards. I mean, it's like I hated that girl after making out with her, and it totally hurt my spiritual life. It hurt me a lot.

Sleuth: How do you think girls feel when they realize that you just played a game with them? The one night stand?

Ken: I think girls are kind of brokenhearted because I think they expect something more. I think that they get some idea in their head that they're going to be boyfriend-girlfriend. Girls are more romantic than guys are. But the guy feels lousy too; he feels like dirt afterwards. He's ashamed of it.

Sleuth: Have you ever been used by your friends?

All: Yeah.

Ken: Like at lunch time and someone comes and says, "Hey, let me have one of your Twinkies or half a sandwich." Two weeks later you're sitting there with your lunch and the guy has a gourmet meal and says, "Hey,

(Continued on other side.)

get outa here, man, I don't know you," you know?

Tom: I've had friends where we've been doing something, just little pranks and stuff, and they would say, "Go ahead, do it," and you'd go do it and they'd say, "I didn't do it."

Sleuth: They used you as bait.

Tom: Yeah, they get you to do it, and then when it comes to getting busted, "I don't even know him," you know.

Sleuth: Have you ever been used by someone who just wanted to use your brains for the answers on a test?

Jennifer: A person that never sits by you or talks to you or anything comes up to you and says, "Hi, how are you today?" and they bring their little paper and stuff. Giving you little plans and signals from them so that they can copy from you.

Kathy: Someone comes up desperately saying, "I need the answers to this test and if I don't get them I'll fail this class." And you say, "I don't want to make this kid flunk the class."

Sleuth: What would you normally say? Would you give in?

Kathy: It depends on if they studied.

Patti: They'd say, "I studied."

Linda: Sometimes you feel real bad.

Jennifer: Yeah, if it's your friend, you feel guilty and you will give them the answers.

Linda: It's not right, we're not supposed to be helping them out.

Kathy: You know, I used some people for their homework. I've never really thought about it before. I'd go up and say, "Hi, how ya doin'?" and I'd ask them for the answers and get them and walk off. And I never really realized it until right now!

Ken: When you're old enough maybe get a job and help them out.

Patti: Not talking back to them, respecting them.

Sleuth: How would you show a friend at school that you were really a friend and that you weren't really using them like a disposal?

Jennifer: Just being really sweet and sending them little cards and talking to them.

Linda: Be yourself.

Sleuth: Do you ever use your parents?

Tom: Yeah, like Mom's easy. I won't ask Dad for the 10 bucks, I'll ask Mom. You watch TV with her, whatever she's watching, you ask how she's doing.

Mack: She says, "What do you want, what do you want?"

Sleuth: How could you show your parents that you're not just using them?

Linda: Help them around the house with housework.

Sleuth: If you were going to give a little advice to others about using people what would you tell them?

Tom: If you use someone, most often you end up hurting them.

Mack: Not only can you hurt them but you also hurt yourself.

Patti: I didn't really think anyone could use me, but now I would know from my experiences. A lot of kids don't know because they haven't really experienced it yet.

Bob: You've heard it before, you've heard it from your mom and dad. If you hurt them, you hurt yourself.

Ken: They get really calloused and insensitive.

Sleuth: What happens to a person who is a continual user?

Bob: They end up with no friends.

DAILY NUGGETS

Day 1 Read Romans 15:1-3. What should we try to do for others?

Day 2 Philippians 2:4-11. List some of Christ's attitudes that we can imitate.

Day 3 2 Corinthians 5:14,15. According to these verses, who should Christians serve?

Day 4 2 Timothy 3:1-5. In your Bible, circle the nasty behavior that you have seen going on around you.

Day 5 Galatians 5:16,17. By what source of power should we live?

Day 6 Galatians 2:20. Try rewriting this classic verse in your own words.

THEME: Respect for others.

Session 12

BIBLE STUDY OUTLINE

Read Philippians 2:1-4, making the following points as time allows.

Verses 1-4: This passage simply means that we should always show respect for each other. As verse 2 says, we should be like-minded. That doesn't mean we should always act, think and look the same—it means we should have the common goal of working together and caring for each other. That's part of showing respect for one another. Verse 3 states that we must put other people before ourselves. And verse 4 tells us to keep an eye on the interests and needs of our friends.

All of these things are against our old, sinful human nature. Until Christ gets hold of us and changes our attitudes, we tend to put ourselves first. We look out for our own interests before those of our friends and we often have a hard time working together in unity. But Jesus can change all of that. With His help, and following His example, we can learn to show respect for others by being like-minded and united.

NOTES

OBJECT LESSON: FLASHLIGHT BATTERIES

Show a flashlight to your students—the kind that requires two batteries. Be sure the batteries are fresh so that the light is bright. As you speak about unity and like-mindedness, put the two batteries into the flashlight. But turn one battery around so that it is placed the wrong way. The flashlight won't work. Pretend to be a bit mystified. Remove the batteries, reveal the problem and correctly reassemble the flashlight. Turn it on and shine it for all to see.

Say something like, **When the batteries are not working together, the flashlight is dead. When the batteries are like-minded and united, so to speak, the light shines brightly. In the same way, only when the members of this group are like-minded and united in their respect for God and for each other can the spiritual light shine for all to see.**

DISCUSSION QUESTIONS

1. **Respect is one of those seemingly odd words we seldom use—well, maybe your folks shove it at you now and then. But what does it really mean to someone your age?**

2. **If you want someone to treat you with respect, what should they do?**

3. **If you want someone to treat you with respect, what can you do to earn their respect?**

4. **We said that being like-minded doesn't mean we should always act, think and look alike. It means we should have the common goal of working together and caring for each other. How does this relate to respect? What are some things we as a group should be working together to accomplish?**

Things to do with calculator paper.

PEANUT RACES

Fold calculator paper lengthwise to form a trough for a peanut race. Trough should be 15 feet or longer. Each team holds the trough as shown, moving it as necessary to get the peanut to tumble from one end to the other. Trough may not be raised above any player's waist. A dropped peanut must be started over.

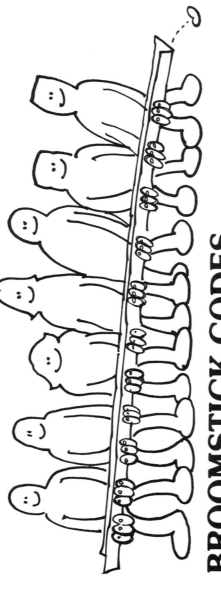

BROOMSTICK CODES

Roll calculator paper around a broomstick as shown. Write a message on the paper. Remove the paper and mail it to a student or allow teams to try to decode it. Be sure to give instructions on how to decode the message. The paper must be rewrapped around a broomstick.

WRITE YOUR MESSAGE HERE.

INSIGHTS FOR THE LEADER

WHAT THE SESSION IS ABOUT

A review of scriptural principles about relationships.

SCRIPTURE STUDIED

Scripture from previous sessions.

KEY PASSAGE

"The only thing that counts is faith expressing itself through love"
Galatians 5:6

AIMS OF THE SESSION

During this session your learners will:
1. Read selected Scriptures from previous sessions;
2. Review practical applications of scriptural instructions about relationships;
3. Evaluate their spiritual progress.

This is a special session designed to review the course content.

The session is centered on "The Game of G.O.M.," which will give students an opportunity to review past themes, reread some of the important Bible passages from the sessions and evaluate their growth in the area of relationships.

As you prepare for this session, review the other twelve sessions to refresh your recall of the Bible content and your students' responses. (If you have not taught all of the sessions, prepare by reading the introductory material at the beginning of each session.)

Plan to make the session a relaxed time. You might even want to decorate the room as for a party and provide refreshments at the beginning or the end of the session.

While learners play the "Game of G.O.M." (which stands for "God, Others, Me"), circulate around the room and tune in on what they are saying. Spend some time talking informally with learners who finish early about what they liked most and least about this course. Listen especially for what they remember the most and why it made an impression on them. The more you learn about your students, the better you will be able to minister to them. If students are willing, provide a time for sharing insights gained during this quarter.

NOTES

SESSION PLAN

BEFORE CLASS BEGINS: Photocopy "The Game of G.O.M." Teaching Resource pages. The game is printed on two separate sheets of paper which must be taped together to form the whole game board. You will need one "Game of G.O.M." game board for every four students. You will also need to cut apart the numbers from the third Teaching Resource page (photocopy first, if necessary) and place one set in a container for each team. Or use a game die for each team. If you wish, provide small awards for winners of the game. There is no Gateway worksheet for this session.

Step 1 (2-3 minutes): Have students form groups of four (or less if necessary). Distribute the game boards and other needed materials. Tell students to read the instructions found on the game board. Answer any questions students may have about the game.

Step 2 (time is variable): Have students play "The Game of G.O.M." for the amount of time available. If your time is limited, the winner will be the person on each team whose marker is nearest to the goal when you stop the play. If more time is available, students may be able to play the game several times, perhaps switching teams each time.

For added fun you can have small awards available for the winners.

While students are playing, circulate among the groups to answer questions and to listen to students' responses.

Step 3 (2-3 minutes): Wrap up this review session by saying something like this: **We have read a number of Scriptures as we have played the Game of G.O.M. Think back over the verses you read during the game and pick out the one that means the most to you.**

Step 4 (5-10 minutes): Ask for volunteers to state the verses they have selected. You might want to begin by sharing the verse that is most meaningful to you. As students share their verses, make brief comments about the Scripture's applications to daily living (your review of the session contents will help you here). Or ask the students to explain why the verse is meaningful or how it could be lived out in a practical way in daily life.

Step 5 (time is variable): Serve refreshments if you have planned to do so. Spend some time informally getting to know your students better and allowing them to know you on a personal basis.

Close in prayer.

Distribute the Fun Page as students leave.

The Game of G.O.M.
(God, Others, Myself).   For 2, 3 or 4 players.

■ Rules:

You need: One marker for each player (a coin, piece of old gum or whatever), a pencil, numbered slips of paper provided by your teacher (which are shuffled and placed facedown in a pile) or a game die.

To begin play: Starting from the Heart, each player selects a numbered card from the stack and moves his or her marker the number of spaces indicated. A player may move forward or backward, but not both ways in the same move.

The object: To capture the Treasures by landing on them. When a player lands on a Treasure, he or she writes his or her initials by the Treasure. One player may not land on a Treasure while another player is on it, but all players may land on any of the Treasures one at a time.

Once a player has captured all four Treasures, he or she returns as quickly as possible to the Heart. The first player to do so wins. However, players may not pass each other, except on the Passing Squares. If a player is blocked, he or she must reverse direction or wait until the path is clear. Players must follow the instructions on each square they land on.

You may pass each other only on these Passing Squares.

SOLID GOLD ROCK of a relationship with Christ.

Rubies of a CHRISTLIKE ATTITUDE towards others.

You try to treat all people fairly (see Matt. 5:46,47). Go to the nearest Treasure.

You try to help people fit in with your group of friends. Go ahead two spaces.

You gripe because God gave you curly hair. Lose one turn.

You realize that God made you special (see Psalm 139). Go ahead one space.

You rely totally on Christ to rescue you (see Eph. 2:8,9). Take another turn.

You complain that the church is boring (but you don't help). Follow the arrow.

Your spiritual life is like a yo-yo. Follow the arrow.

You stand firm in the faith. Advance three spaces.

You try to impress God with good works. Lose one turn.

You act like a fool at a party. Lose a turn.

You lose your temper with your friends. Lose one turn.

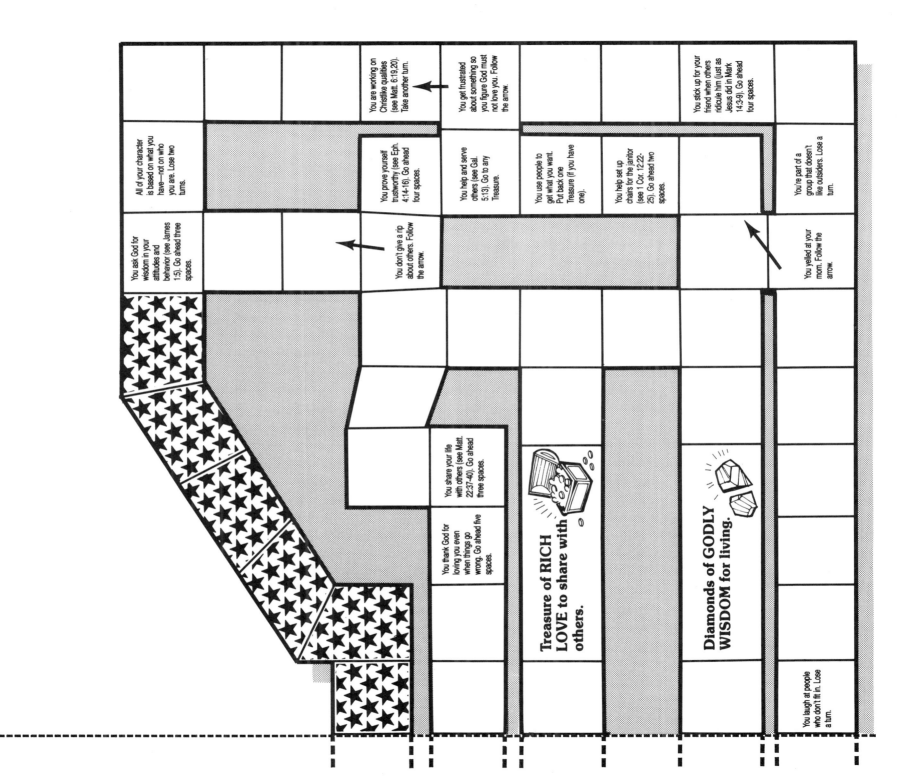

You are working on Christlike qualities (see Matt. 6:19,20). Take another turn.

You get frustrated about something so you figure God must not love you. Follow the arrow.

You stick up for your friend when others ridicule him (just as Jesus did in Mark 14:3-9). Go ahead four spaces.

All of your character is based on what you have—not on who you are. Lose two turns.

You prove yourself trustworthy (see Eph. 4:14-16). Go ahead four spaces.

You help and serve others (see Gal. 5:13). Go to any Treasure.

You use people to get what you want. Put back one Treasure (if you have one).

You help set up chairs for the janitor (see 1 Cor. 12:22-25). Go ahead two spaces.

You're part of a group that doesn't like outsiders. Lose a turn.

You ask God for wisdom in your attitudes and behavior (see James 1:5). Go ahead three spaces.

You don't give a rip about others. Follow the arrow.

You yelled at your mom. Follow the arrow.

You share your life with others (see Matt. 22:37-40). Go ahead three spaces.

Treasure of RICH LOVE to share with others.

Diamonds of GODLY WISDOM for living.

You thank God for loving you even when things go wrong. Go ahead five spaces.

You laugh at people who don't fit in. Lose a turn.

1	2	3	4	5	6
1	2	3	4	5	6
1	2	3	4	5	6
1	2	3	4	5	6
1	2	3	4	5	6

SPECIAL EDITION
The Sleuth looks at
RELATIONSHIPS!

We all have relationships. Relationships with ourselves, our parents, our friends, our Lord, and so on. Some relationships are good— sometimes, some are not so good!

And sometimes, some are like these:

RELATIONSHIPS WITH OURSELVES: SELF-IMAGE

The way it is:

The way you think it really is:

The way you'd like it to be:

WOW! AN EIGHTH GRADER WITH A MUSTACHE!

TALENTS AND ABILITIES

The way it really is:

HAPPY TRAILS TO YOU, UNTIL WE MEET AGAIN...

PLINK! TINK!

ROY ROGERS CRANK GUITAR

The way you'd like it to be:

MUSHROOMS MAKE MEEEEE GAG, BABY!

SO HOT!

TWAK! BAA!

The way it should be:

STRUM!

RELATIONSHIPS WITH OUR PARENTS: HOW WE GET ALONG

The way they think it is:

DANGER WILD ANIMAL!

The way you think it is:

IMPRISONED

The way it should be:

ALLOWANCE

The way they think it is:

SAY G'BYE!

24K

The way you think it is:

HELP! MY PARENTS ARE CHEAP!

ALMS FOR THE POOR

The way you'd like it to be:

$ $ $

RELATIONSHIPS WITH FRIENDS: LUNCH-TIME FRIENDS

The way it should be:

The way you think it is:

The way it really is:

RELATIONSHIPS WITH GOD: TIME IN PRAYER

The way it should be:

The way you see it:

The way God sees it:

RELATIONSHIPS AT JUNIOR HIGH BIBLE STUDY:

The way it should be:

The way it really is:

Another way it really is:

AND FINALLY . . .

The way it should be:

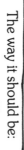

The way you see it:

The way it usually turns out:

Yep! We all must relate to the people around us.

There is one key word that should apply to every relationship we have. It's written in the Bible verse on my note pad there. Can you find the word?

The Sleuth

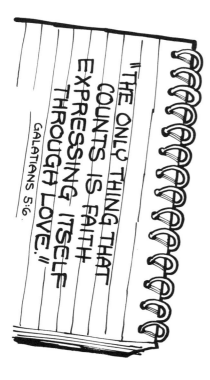

"THE ONLY THING THAT COUNTS IS FAITH EXPRESSING ITSELF THROUGH LOVE."

— GALATIANS 5:6

THE COMPLETE JUNIOR HIGH BIBLE STUDY RESOURCE BOOK #5
© 1988 GL/LIGHT FORCE, VENTURA, CA 93006

THEME: Accept and help each other—that's what relationships are for.

Session 13

BIBLE STUDY OUTLINE

The passage you'll review is Romans 15:1-7. The following points will help your listeners grasp the meaning of God's Word.

Verse 1: Paul says that "we who are strong ought to bear with the failings of the weak." By "we who are strong," he means spiritually strong. Spiritual strength is developed by a close relationship to God. We develop this closeness by trusting God for the things we need, by prayer, fellowship and Bible study. It takes a full-time commitment. Bearing with the failings of others means more than just putting up with those people. Like holding a baby in one's arms, bearing means to lovingly uphold.

Verse 2: The purpose of pleasing others is to build them up spiritually. It's much easier to become a strong Christian when you are involved with a strong group of believers. If you feel that you are a weak Christian, hang out with strong believers. Soon your spiritual pilot light will flare into brightness.

Verse 3: This verse quotes Psalm 69:9. It could be rewritten like this: "The insults of those who insult God have fallen on Jesus." Jesus did not seek to please Himself, but voluntarily took man's abuse aimed at God. Christ is our example. We should also seek to build unselfish relationships with others and help them in their Christian walk.

Verses 4-6: Paul encourages us to have a spirit of unity as we follow Christ. It makes sense that if we are all seeking to be united with Christ, we will become united with each other. Again, it's difficult to be a strong Christian all by yourself. Like a log that falls off a pile of burning wood, you'll soon grow cold. Together, we can burn brightly and glorify God. (At this point, do the Verbal Illustration.)

Verse 7: The whole purpose, then, to bearing each other's failings, pleasing each other, being united and accepting each other is to bring praise to God. He is honored by groups of Christians who care for each other.

VERBAL ILLUSTRATION: PEOPLE GOING PLACES

Tell your students something like this: **Have you ever been on a large airplane? Everyone is packed into their seats. They are all heading for the same airport. For the moment, they all have the same purpose and goal. They are united—but they are not uniform. Each person is different. They look different, talk differently, probably think differently. Once they reach the airport they will go their separate ways. You can see the same thing on a crowded highway. Everyone is going the same way, hopefully, but each person is a unique individual.**

Christian unity is kind of like that. We are united in our goals and purpose—but there's room for us to have our own personalities. God doesn't require uniformity. In fact, He desires each one of us to be involved in serving this group because we each have different gifts and abilities.

Return to the Bible Study Outline.

DISCUSSION QUESTIONS

1. **What are some of the hard things about Christianity that some of us might fail at? How can we work together as a group to succeed?**

2. **Why is it wise to hang out with strong Christians? What should you do if you're with a group that is only Christian in church and worldly the rest of the time?**

3. **How does unity differ from uniformity?**

4. **How does accepting people bring praise to God?**

THE COMPLETE
JUNIOR HIGH BIBLE STUDY
RESOURCE BOOK #5

Simple discussion starters for times when you don't have time to prepare.

CONCORDANCE HOP

Allow someone to select any word listed in a concordance, and then have everyone look up all the verses listed under that word. We suggest you use a short concordance at the back of a Bible to avoid overly lengthy lists of verses. The word to look up can be chosen randomly by asking the student to close his or her eyes while pointing at the page.

QUESTION NIGHT

If you feel you can stand up to the challenge, sponsor an "Ask Any Question Night." Students are allowed to express their questions about Christianity, the Bible and life.

WHAT'S BEST?

Ask your listeners to identify their favorite TV shows, songs, movies and so forth. Lead a discussion based on why the students picked what they did, what are the good and bad points of their favorites, and so on.

CLIP ART
AND OTHER GOODIES

The following pages contain all sorts of fun, high quality clip art. Put it to good use: brighten up your youth group's mail outs, bulletins, posters and overhead transparencies. Cut 'em out, paste 'em up, run 'em off and there you have it!

You'll be happy to know that the LIGHT FORCE publishes several great clip art books for youth workers. These books are the finest on the market. They are made by youth workers for youth workers. Available at your local Christian supply store, or write

THE LIGHT FORCE
P.O. BOX 6309
OXNARD, CA 93031

WANT TO PRODUCE GREAT PROMOTIONAL MATERIAL?

TURN THE PAGE FOR EASY INSTRUCTIONS . . .

EASY INSTRUCTIONS

1. **Get a sheet of clean white paper. This will be the master for your promotional piece.**

2. **Choose the art you want from this section. Cut it out and glue it to the master.**

3. **Add headlines with rub-on letters (available at any art store) or with a felt pen. Add body copy with a typewriter or by hand. (Type on a separate sheet and cut and paste.)**

4. **Run off as many copies as you need, hand them out or drop them in the mail.   Presto!**

TIPS:

Go heavy on the artwork, light on the copy. A piece with too many words goes unread.

Get in the habit of making a monthly calendar of events. It doesn't have to be an expensive masterpiece; just so it tells your group members what they can find at your church.

Print the calendar on the back of the **Gateway** student worksheet. This will insure that these pages are saved and read.

The Mug File

The information on this sheet will be treated as privileged (which means it's a privilege to have it and we won't go pasting it up on the walls). Please answer honestly and completely. Thanks.

Name _____

Address _____

Phone _____ Grade in school _____

Age _____ Birth date _____ Name of school _____

1. How long have you been coming to this church?

2. Who do you come with?

3. What's your favorite sport to participate in?

4. What is your favorite hobby or pastime?

5. Name your favorite music band or performer.

6. What is your favorite TV show?

7. Name your three best friends.

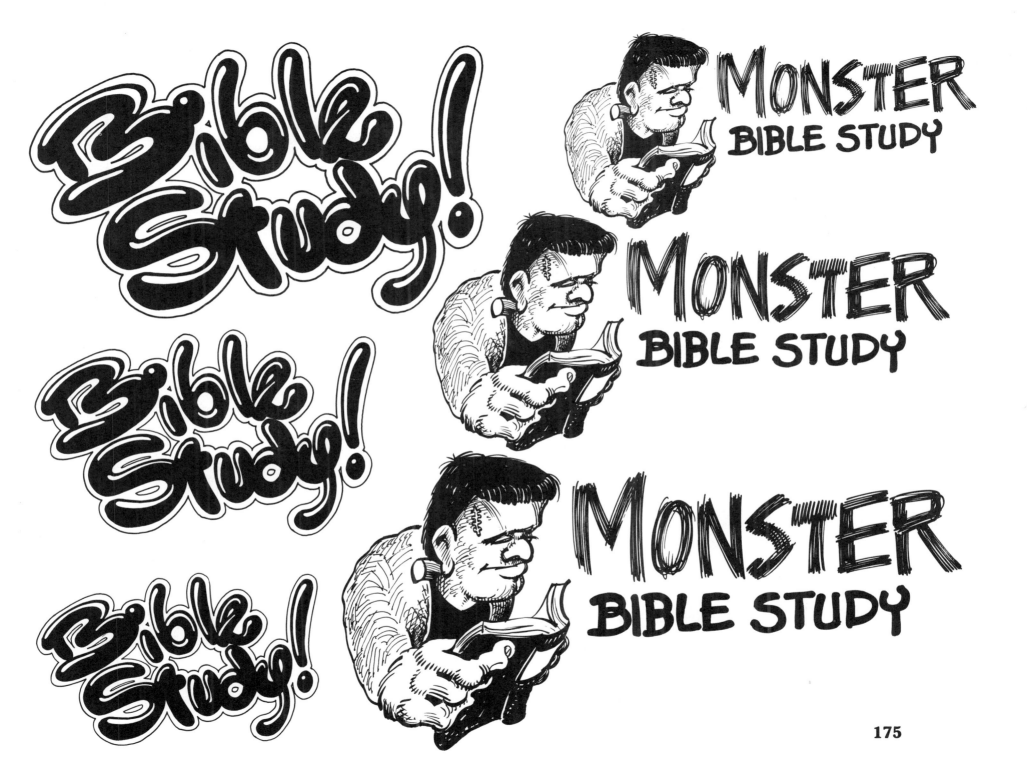

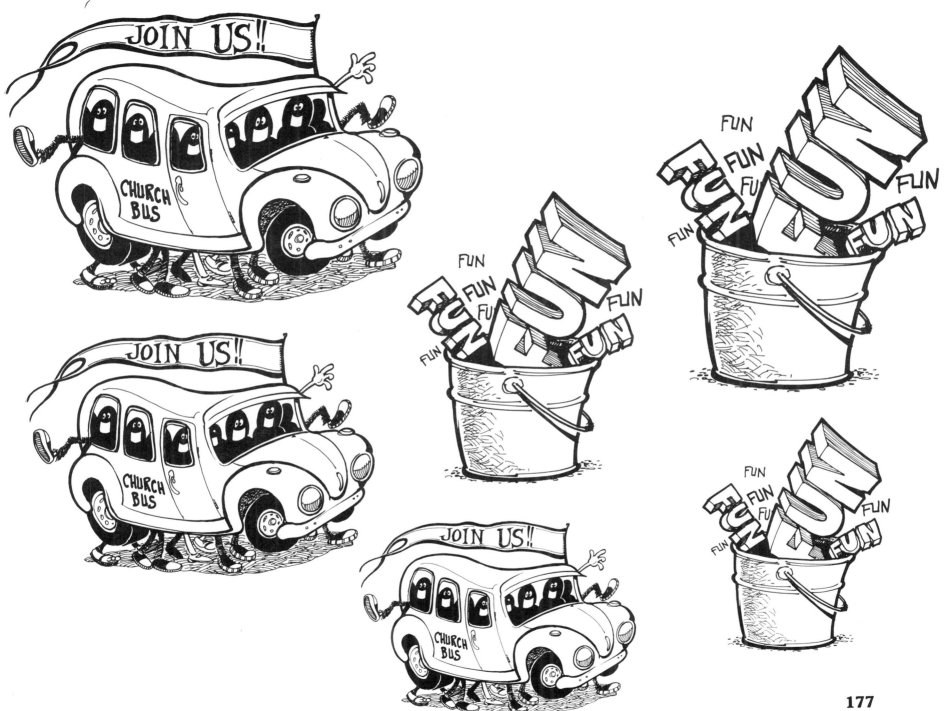

HIGH VOLTAGE HAPPENINGS!

HIGH VOLTAGE HAPPENINGS!

HIGH VOLTAGE HAPPENINGS!

BIKE
HIKE

BIKE
HIKE

BIKE
HIKE

BIG PICNIC!

BIG PICNIC!

183